D0387151

Discarded from
Garfield County Public
Library System

GARFIELD COUNTY LIBRARIES
Carbondale Branch Library
320 Sopris Ave
Carbondale, CO 81623
(970) 963-2889 – Fax (970) 963-8573
www.gcpld.org

The Secret of "The Secret"

Garfield County Libraries

The SECRET *of* "THE SECRET"

Unlocking the Mysteries of the Runaway Bestseller

KAREN KELLY

THOMAS DUNNE BOOKS

St. Martin's Press 🐾 New York

THOMAS DUNNE BOOKS.
An imprint of St. Martin's Press.

THE SECRET OF "THE SECRET." Copyright © 2007 by Karen Kelly.
All rights reserved. Printed in the United States of America.
No part of this book may be used or reproduced in any manner whatsoever
without written permission except in the case of brief quotations
embodied in critical articles or reviews. For information, address
St. Martin's Press, 175 Fifth Avenue, New York, N.Y. 10010.

ISBN-13: 978-0-312-37790-8
ISBN-10: 0-312-37790-8

First Edition: August 2007

10 9 8 7 6 5 4 3 2 1

To my father, William H. Kelly,
who advised me to never bet on a horse
I did not believe would win.

Contents

❧

There's something about a secret that makes people want to believe.

— GRAHAM GREENE,
Our Man in Havana (film version)

The Secret of "The Secret"

Introduction

The Secret Is Out

The Secret began as a documentary made by Australian TV producer Rhonda Byrne, which she then followed with a book of the same name. First, I'll let the Secret out of the bag if you haven't already heard what it is, and chances are you have: It's the law of attraction, an idea that has been around for a long time, which posits the concept that you can reach any goal, acquire anything you want, and attain perfect health by thinking positive thoughts about whatever your heart desires. Like attracts like— by thinking negatively, you attract the negativity to you. Think positively about a desire, and you attract that. It's actually not quite that simple, as we'll learn. But for the moment, let's stick with the "101" definition.

On March 2, 2007, the publisher of *The Secret* (Atria Books/ Beyond Words Publishing) announced that it had ordered another print run of the book—nothing new for books that sit on national bestseller lists for several weeks. What astonished the industry was the number of books being printed: 2 million. This was reported to be the largest single reprint in the history of Simon & Schuster, the book's distributor and owner of the Atria imprint. It was certainly unheard of for Beyond Words, the small press that acquired the book. The new print run brought the official number in print in the United States to 3.75 million. In addition, the audio version of the book and the DVD version of the film also sit on top of the bestseller lists. Extending the reach of *The Secret* even more, publishers in twenty countries have bought rights to the book.

Google *The Secret* and 264 million entries come up. Among them are Web sites of hundreds of life coaches, spiritual gurus, and alternative medicine practitioners who advertise *Secret* seminars, sessions, and advice, often using the same typeface and logo that adorns the book and movie packaging. Bloggers dissect the messages in the film and book. Scores of supporters and detractors from all over the country, if not the world, post online testimonials to *The Secret*'s power as well as criticisms of what some say is its problematic focus on materialism. Established newspapers, magazines, and television shows ranging from *The Wall Street Journal* to *Newsweek, Oprah, Larry King Live, Fox & Friends,* and even the serious news–oriented *Nightline* have done pieces on the book. A search of LexisNexis, the online archive of newspaper and magazine content, shows that more than 150 articles (both pro and con) have been written about *The Secret* in newspapers and magazines since its publication in November 2006. Blogger Russell Portwood wrote an online exposé of *The Secret* as a way of marketing his own success products (www .zwebber.com/thesecret/exposed.pdf). Several book publishers are putting out their own law of attraction manuals. And that's just the tip of the iceberg. All this attention adds up to a worldwide phenomenon. So what's all the fuss about?

That's the question I set out to answer, and the result is this book.

When something stirs the masses, it's *not* trivial—it means something. During my undergraduate days as an anthropology student in the late 1970s, and as a film studies student in graduate school in the early 1980s, studying pop culture in an academic setting was de rigueur. I learned to appreciate the comings and goings of trends without feeling above them (I'm not, and neither are you). Take a closer look at a singular event such as the bally-hoo surrounding *The Secret,* and you get a better understanding of the world you live in, and of yourself, for that matter. That has certainly been my experience working on this book, and I hope it is yours in reading it.

For example, I recited the mantra "The pencil skirt will zip up" twenty to thirty times before heading to my closet. Is this the real reason my ridiculously narrow Jil Sander skirt fits me or is it because I have been literally working my butt off on the elliptical machine at the Y? Regardless, I will never put that skirt on without first going through my positive thinking paces, lest my thighs bust the delicate seams.

My skirt experiment is one reason why my intention is not to debunk *The Secret* or put it down in any way—nor is it to sing its praises and encourage everyone to drop what they're doing and start visualizing the riches we all doubtless deserve. There are some very smart, decent people on both sides of *The Secret*'s argument, and I will let several share fascinating, useful insights here. I've approached my inquiry in a sober-minded, respectful fashion, but let's face it—no line of questioning that walks the fine line between reality and the paranormal can be approached without some humor.

The result of the journey I went on is my well-researched

explanation for how *The Secret* gained such momentum, what its flaws and features are, where it comes from, and whether or not the people Byrne claims lived by "the Secret" really did. To make my argument easily digestible, *The Secret of "The Secret"* is organized into three sections.

Part I defines and examines the "Secret Phenomenon." Publishing experts, culture watchers, and journalists weigh in on why the movie, the book, and the *idea* struck a chord with the public and how it relates to the current social and political climate in the country. Here's a clue: It might be Bush's fault, but then again, it might not be.

Part II takes a stab at unearthing the historical, scientific, and theological evidence, which the author says supports and even proves that the law of attraction works. I talked to several sincere, reasonable people featured in *The Secret,* as well as open-minded theologians, quantum physicists, brain scientists, psychologists, and other academics who were not featured in the book or the movie but were brave enough to return my phone calls and e-mails and consent to an interview. I got the brush-off from some; others never responded to my polite requests for a little time (I took silence as a no). It's amazing to me how many professors of popular culture, American studies, and film studies turned me down because they had never heard of *The Secret.* Shouldn't even a dim awareness of what's going on be part of their job description?

Part III checks out thirteen historical figures who are mentioned in *The Secret* as using the law of attraction—from Ludwig van Beethoven and William Shakespeare to Thomas Edison and Andrew Carnegie—even if they didn't really *know* it, as Rhonda Byrne asserts. ("People who have drawn wealth into their lives used The Secret, whether consciously or unconsciously," she writes.) I look at what is known about these individuals in terms of their philosophies, beliefs, and religious convictions in order to reveal how the law of attraction may or may not have played a role in their work and lives. It's actually surprising—Beethoven had books on his shelves that could be defined as metaphysical. Whether or not these books had anything to do with his success is another matter. Self-consciously short, pockmarked, and envious of the royals, Beethoven certainly was not given to pure optimism. Plus, he had talent.

My conclusion—well, you have to flip ahead to the end of the book to find out. But I'll give you a clue (or three!) here, beautifully captured by P. T. Barnum (a figure not mentioned anywhere in *The Secret*), and I am *not* referring to his most famous line ("There's a sucker born every minute."):

1. "Without promotion something terrible happens—nothing!"
2. "More persons, on the whole, are humbugged by believing in nothing than by believing too much."
3. "Those who really desire to attain an independence, have only to set their minds upon it, and adopt the proper means, as they do in regard to any other object which they wish to accomplish, and the thing is easily done."

I'd like to think that Barnum, a showman and well-known debunker of false claims, but also a master of making money, would appreciate *The Secret* for two reasons: its ability to capture and seduce the American public's imagination; and its core philosophy that you can do anything if you set your mind to it, which includes making money. After all, in 1880 Barnum wrote his own self-help guide to acquiring wealth: *Art of Money Getting* (downloadable for free at www.deceptionary.com/ftp/PTBarnum.pdf). Ironically, the formula Barnum prescribes mirrors the journey Rhonda Byrne seems to have traveled with her *Secret*. It's the high road, and I'll take you on it.

Part I

WHY THE SECRET, AND WHY NOW?

The Secret's path to bestseller lists and into consumers' homes is at once traditional and completely contemporary. Like many bestsellers and top-grossing movies, it is beautifully made, attractively packaged, and marketed well. It has a great "why to buy" promise that generated huge interest and sales. What's new is that it has used a convergence of databases, Internet marketing, lightning-speed word of mouth, and "viral" communication to spread the word. And there's something else contributing to its success, according to experts from media, psychology, and science: The timing is right.

A perfect storm of social and economic forces, not to mention a general angst within the public, meant that by the time 2006 turned into 2007, we were perfectly poised to embrace *The Secret*. Plus, unbridled enthusiasm and rose-colored-glasses optimism aren't new to us. Americans are the most hopeful people on earth. Any book that promises lifelong happiness (without really trying) cannot be considered without looking at the history of self-help tomes that came before—and there are loads of them. The thing is, if the advice in these books was all absolute bunk, why do they keep selling? I'm not so cynical that I believe it's simply because we are gullible. There just might be something to the idea behind *The Secret*.

· 1 ·

From Down Under to On Top:
How the Secret Spread

IT'S TOO SOON to tell whether or not *The Secret* book will make the list of bestselling titles of all time, which is a very high bar to reach considering that those at the *bottom* of the list have sold nearly 30 million copies. Books at the top of the list include everything from the Bible (50 to 60 billion) and *Quotations from Chairman Mao Zedong* (900 million—but he had a built-in audience) to *Harry Potter and the Philosopher's Stone* (107 million) and Richard Bach's *Jonathan Livingston Seagull* (40 million). (The numbers are from Wikipedia.com and Amazon.com.) Yet *The Secret* is heading in the right direction, with nearly 4 million copies in print. People who do not work in the publishing industry sometimes misunderstand what big print numbers actually mean—and what an accomplishment it is to achieve sales of even 100,000, let alone a million. Most books are lucky to make sales in the five-figure range.

"Writers are up against the 200,000 books that are published each year. One year the publishers will say, 'Too many books,' so they cut back to 195,000 a year," explains Constance Sayre, a principal in the publishing consultancy Market Partners International. Added to that, she says, new authors are also facing the fact that independent booksellers "are dying like flies and the chain booksellers' sales are dropping." The book itself is up against various forms of electronic media, which is why Sayre and others in the business say that the *The Secret* DVD made such a huge difference; otherwise, it is hard to get anyone to pay attention. Indeed, there would have been no book without the movie—it is a direct result of the DVD's popularity and of its actual content (most of the book is a transcription of what the experts said).

Both DVD and book aroused a lot of debate and complaint (which is not to say that the Bible and *Harry Potter* haven't—of course they have). Yet the story surrounding Byrne's book, its marketing, and the inevitable criticism and discussion that generally follow are what cultural studies professors call part of its "production"—the more people talk about something, the longer it exists. The story of how it came into being, which by now has become a mini-legend, offers lessons in publishing, Internet marketing, convergence culture, optimism, cynicism, collective unconscious, and wishful thinking.

Inspiration and Origins

The law of attraction is not new, and it's been called many different things over the years: positive thinking, psychology, flow, faith, the power of intention, or the law of abundance. It even has an opposite: Murphy's law. So was Rhonda Byrne simply rehashing an age-old idea, one that had appeared several times before in books and even movies? When *New York Times* reporter Allen Salkin asked Byrne about the Secret business, because it seemed like hocus-pocus, she said, "No, no, no, if you look at *The Master Key System,* it was very expensive knowledge to buy and was subscription only." Byrne was referring to Charles Haanel's twenty-four-week success program, which was originally published in 1912 and cost around $1,500—a royal sum at the time. It is widely available in inexpensive book form today, and I even found a free Internet version. Apparently, Byrne believed that although the law of attraction wasn't new, compiling the ideas in an easy-to-digest and readily available format was groundbreaking.

According to the official Web site of *The Secret,* www.thesecret .tv, Byrne's version, which was first articulated as a DVD, came about "on a spring day toward the end of 2004." This may seem contradictory to those of us in the Western Hemisphere, where winter ends the year, but Byrne's home base is in Australia, which is in the Eastern Hemisphere, where the seasons are reversed. On this particular day, the fifty-something mother of two was in the midst of a personal and financial crisis, which she recounted on an episode of *Oprah.* According to Byrne, her daughter, Hayley, gave her a copy of self-help writer Wallace D. Wattles's *The Science of Getting Rich,* originally published in 1910 and still in print today.

Wattles's book explains the secret laws of the universe—and most primarily, the law of attraction—in this way: "A thought, in this substance, produces the thing that is imagined by the thought." Wattles repeats this idea in various ways throughout his book: "There is a thinking stuff from which all things are made, and which, in turn, in its original state, permeates, penetrates, and fills the interspaces of the universe. A thought, in this substance, produces the thing that is imagined by the thought." But it's not so simple: "To think according to appearance is easy," he writes; "to think truth regardless of appearances is laborious, and requires expenditure of more power than any other workman is called upon to perform."

More about Wattles later, but for now, it's notable that these quotes unmistakably mirror what *The Secret* says, and the similarities suggest Byrne did indeed read Wattles and drew upon his ideas. However, most books about the law of attraction say generally pretty much the same thing, so there is some debate about whether it was Wattles's book alone that inspired Byrne to create her documentary. And that's where this part of the story becomes interesting.

Reporter Allen Salkin, who wrote about *The Secret* for the *Times,* said that Byrne was "100 percent familiar" not only with other law of attraction books but also with another thematically related film, *What the Bleep Do We Know!?,* a documentary about the science of the mind and the power of consciousness made in 2004 by William Arntz, Betsy Chasse, and Mark Vicente. Salkin describes *The Secret* as "a watered down, Kmart version of *What the Bleep*; you may think you are watching something similar, but *What the Bleep* is much more about science," than spirituality, he says.

"*The Bleep* came out in Australia well before they started to make *The Secret,*" says *Bleep* filmmaker Betsy Chasse, who interviewed one of the producers of *The Secret* DVD and asked him whether or not *What the Bleep* influenced him. "He said it did and it didn't, so obviously it had to have had an effect on the filmmakers. And there's a crossover of people they interviewed," she explained, including physicists Fred Alan Wolf and John Hagelin.

According to the official version of the DVD's inception, published on *The Secret*'s Web site, Byrne dug a little further into the law of attraction and discovered there were people "alive today" who were aware of the information and were in fact writing books and producing tapes and DVDs about it, holding workshops, and traveling around the United States giving speeches about it—rather than hoarding it all for themselves.

Byrne saw a hole in the market, and said she wanted to pull all the bits and pieces of information together in one easily accessible place, first in a documentary—a medium she understood quite well. Part of the secret of the DVD's success is that Byrne is a savvy television producer who knows what she's doing. *The Secret* Web site includes information on her Australian film company, Prime Time Productions, and lists an impressive roster of highly rated reality and documentary-style programs, including *The World's Greatest Commercials* and related specials: "Adults Only," "Cannes," "Funniest Commercials Ever Made," and "SEX SELLS." Another program, *Australia Behaving Badly,* "explores the differences between what Australians say they would do when their conscience is on the line, and what they actually do when faced with temptation." *OZ Encounters,* a one-hour special made for Australian TV, features unexplained phenomena experienced by "everyday" Aussies that range from UFO sightings by entire towns to one-on-one alien abductions.

Since many law of attraction practitioners are in the United States, Byrne headed into the Western Hemisphere to start shooting footage with a range of self-help gurus, a physicist, and some metaphysicists. "*The Secret* is the first time anyone has ever put 24 teachers with their own following together in one movie," says bestselling *Men Are from Mars, Women Are from Venus* author John Gray, who appeared in the DVD. An experienced television producer, Byrne knows what she's doing in terms of appealing to broad public taste. "They are saying the same things in a very uplifting way, and that, along with good graphics, made an impact on people. We are a visual society and watch TV more than we read books; nothing holds our attention for very long, so she put the ideas across with that in mind," says Gray.

Among those experts Byrne enlisted to participate in the DVD were longtime law of attraction teachers Jerry and Esther Hicks. The Hickses are two of the most widely recognized and popular law of attraction speakers today—the equivalent of rock stars in the metaphysical movement—so naturally Byrne sought them out. The couple has been on the road talking and writing about the law of attraction since the late 1980s. They say their messages come from divine guidance via a spirit named Abraham who speaks through Esther (they do not use the term "channel"). Their books *The Law of Attraction,* published by Hay House in September 2006, and an earlier volume, *Ask and It Is Given,* also published by Hay House in October 2005, were both channeled by Abraham.

The Hickses are prolific; over the last twenty years they have produced more than six hundred Abraham-inspired books, workbooks, cards, calendars, cassette tapes, CDs, and DVDs. Byrne sought out the Hickses to participate in the first version of the DVD. In a letter the Hickses sent to friends and colleagues in late 2006 (widely available online by Googling "Jerry and Esther Hicks' letter to friends"), the couple related their dismay with how their participation in the DVD was handled. They consented to participate and signed an agreement with Prime Time Productions, Byrne's company, that would give them a small percentage of the net profits and 10 percent of direct-video sales. Esther's "Abraham voice" ended up being used as narration in the first version of the DVD, but neither Esther nor Jerry appeared on screen.

Raveled Threads

The first version of the DVD was released in March 2006. Something happened between the Hickses and Byrne, and Esther demanded to be cut from the DVD, according to Allen Salkin's *Times* story chronicling the rift, published on February 25, 2007. Esther was upset by the way she was used in the DVD and surprised that she was completely offscreen. Byrne recut the video, adding Esther Hicks's onscreen interviews back in.

But according to their letter, the revised DVD was distributed differently than originally promised (on television and via video sales): Byrne had asked them to revise the contract they had signed to allow for different streams of distribution. Byrne had indeed originally planned to go the traditional television broadcast route, but several sources told me that the programming of the 2006 Winter Olympics got in the way, and she decided instead to make the DVD available online for $4.95 per download view. This turned out to be brilliant marketing.

The parties could not come to an agreement, and Byrne recut the DVD a second time, completely removing Esther's voice and image along with any acknowledgment of her intellectual contribution. To make up for the loss of Esther Hicks, Byrne enlisted Lisa Nichols, an author featured in *Chicken Soup for the African American Soul* (part of the series of books made famous by Jack Canfield, who is also featured in *The Secret*) and Marci Shimoff, a contributor to *Chicken Soup for the Woman's Soul*. (Byrne does thank the Hickses and the teachings of Abraham in the acknowledgment section of the book.)

None of the other participants were paid for their contribution, although they have certainly reaped benefits from being in the DVD, as I describe later on. According to the *Times,* the couple said they earned about $500,000 from sales of the original "Hicks version" of the DVD, but receive nothing directly from sales now that the DVD has been recut.

In their letter, the Hickses maintain that they feel very joyful when they watch the movie, and believe it represents Abraham's law of attraction in a very simple way that allows many people to access it. *The Secret* does offer up the law of attraction's most basic fundamentals, and its optimistic explanation is one aspect of the book that has received criticism by those who have long been familiar with its principles.

Kristine Pidkameny, editor in chief of the One Spirit Book Club and an expert on metaphysical literature, draws a distinction between *The Secret* and the Hickses' work. "The difference is that the Hickses put out pure content—you can listen and watch one of their [video] talks many times and get different things out of it with each new viewing," she says. "*Ask and It Is Given, Amazing Power of Deliberate Intention,* and *The Law of Attraction* are straightforward but multilayered with information. *The Secret* is slicker. During my first viewing, I had to stay open and just say to myself, 'Let me not say this reminds me of other things, and evaluate it clearly.'"

More than one source has told me that the Hickses are not actually as magnanimous as their letter implies. If it is true that they are angrier than they are letting on, and it certainly seems credible, it's hard to blame them; their dignity in being so self-restrained is admirable. Allen Salkin says they are sensitive because they may have felt used by another author, Lynn Grabhorn, who they thought borrowed too liberally from their work without giving them enough credit. Grabhorn was a former advertising professional in New York. She also founded an audiovisual educational company in Los Angeles before moving to Washington state, where she ran a mortgage brokerage. At any rate, she had attended a Hickses seminar sometime in the 1990s and was so impressed with what she heard, according to Allen Salkin, that she approached the couple afterward with an idea. She asked them, "Do you mind if I take this material and turn it into a book?"

It's unclear how the Hickses responded to the question, but Grabhorn felt confident enough to follow through with her idea, and the result is *Excuse Me Your Life Is Waiting: The Astonishing Power of Feelings,* which she originally self-published in the late 1990s and then eventually sold to a small publisher, Hampton Roads, who issued its edition in 1999. Ancillary products and workshops followed, most notably her Life Course 101. "She plagiarized the Hickses, and this is why they were upset with Rhonda. They feel everyone is taking from them," says Salkin.

Grabhorn died in May 5, 2004, so while her Life Course 101 is no longer being offered (according to her Web site) for obvious reasons, her online presence is still active, and Grabhorn's books and products can still be purchased. Since the law of attraction isn't new, the concept is free for anyone to use and interpret. Still, Grabhorn does give a nod to the Hickses in the introduction to the book. In the beginning of the two-page section she describes her spiritual quest to get more out of life. She describes encounters with "learned professors of physics," and of studying "esoteric sciences."

What she writes next is important in understanding why the Hickses, or anyone in their place, would take offense:

Naturally, with my vast knowledge on the subject, when I came across some provincial teachings from this unlettered, unscientific family of teachers, my first impulse was to pooh-pooh the information because of their enormous over-simplification of what I considered to be a rather formidable topic. So it was more than a tad begrudgingly that I agreed to investigate this taped malarkey that a well-meaning friend had ungraciously shoved in my face.

Upon investigation, she discovered that there was substance in what the Hickses were saying, and made a crucial decision: "And so, in my own prosaic words and style I've reissued here the profoundly simple teachings of the Hicks family in Texas.*" The asterisk refers to a footnote at the bottom of the page with a post office box address—for the Hickses, I assume; the annotation simply reads: "PO Box 690070, San Antonio, TX 78296." The Hickses received no compensation from Grabhorn in exchange for her "reissuing."

Excuse Me, Your Life Is Now: Mastering the Law of Attraction, which is authored by another life coach, Doreen Banaszak, carries on the work of Grabhorn. A message from Grabhorn, posted on her Web site (www.lynngrabhorn.com/messagefromlynn.htm), urges readers to continue teaching and using the law of attraction. In a letter to readers, Banaszak describes how the publishers at Hampton Roads asked her to continue Grabhorn's work now that she's gone (www.your-life-is-now.com/aboutlynnandi.html), and refers to being "familiar" with Abraham and the Hickses.

In spite of those who liberally "borrow" and cash in on the Hickses' work, they continue to actively teach their courses across the country, serving and building a large fan base out of a deluxe RV. "The Hickses blow through a town once or twice a year and for many people that one day with Jerry and Esther could be their entire religious observance for a year," says Salkin. One Spirit's Kristine Pidkameny says her book club offers the Hickses' material very successfully. "They are popular with our members. I have never met them personally, but I work with people who know them, and everyone is impressed by their positive focus. They do not let anyone or anything negative enter the picture. They walk the talk."

Once they closed the door on their relationship with Byrne, the producer was free to begin marketing the current version of the DVD unencumbered by contractual worries.

The Miracle of the Market

The success of the DVD, and later the book, are not simply based on the quality and intriguing nature of their content. "It was a marketing coup," says Arielle Ford, who leads The Ford Group, a public relations company that specializes in the metaphysical and inspirational categories. "There are a zillion other books and movies about the law of attraction and Rhonda came in as a TV producer and made it mysterious and positioned it as myth-busting information. It built slowly." The products' victories in the marketplace owe as much to the way the DVD was made available and reached its audience as to the way the book and movie packages were designed. "The way Rhonda crafted it really did make it seem like a secret," says Allen Salkin. "She knows how to fashion a television show; there is a lot of smoke and mirrors in *The Secret*."

According to book-marketing guru John Kremer, author of *1001 Ways to Market Your Book*, *The Secret* found its audience in a way that is unconventional for most metaphysical and New Age books. "Almost every bestseller in the self-help spiritual categories, all those on the *New York Times* list for the last twenty years, are there because the author has gone out and tirelessly spoken. In this case, the author has not actively done that. Instead she created a viral campaign for the DVD, and built interest for the book in that way. No question it broke the rules."

Its promotion is what will likely become a classic example of how to take a topic that was previously of interest mostly to a niche group of people and make it appealing to the general public—many of whom were previously uninterested in or unfamiliar with this type of New Age thinking or, as it is more commonly referred to nowadays, metaphysics. Metaphysics is a legitimate line of academic inquiry—the study of the nature and interconnectedness of all things—but it has been appropriated by New Age thinkers for more spiritual purposes. It's an eclectic category that encompasses health, medicine, philosophy, psychology, multiculturalism, and a mix of religious beliefs.

Paul H. Ray and Sherry Ruth Anderson called people interested in metaphysics "cultural creatives" in their landmark 2001 book of the same name. They contend that about 26 percent of the population fit the category, which includes people who care deeply about the environment, relationships, social justice, self-actualization, creativity, and spirituality. Gaiam, a Colorado-based company, creates products and information specifically geared to cultural creatives and the mind-body-spirit market. The firm coined the acronym LOHAS for people who follow lifestyles of health and sustainability.

These people were the first and primary market for the DVD version of *The Secret*. Byrne had a direct line to them via the databases of the people who appeared in her DVD. "Basically, it started with the gurus marketing the movie to their own lists," says Salkin. In newsletters and e-mail messages, DVD participants such as Jack Canfield, Ben Johnson, and John Demartini would alert their fans and followers that they were featured in the DVD. "Rhonda had twenty-four teachers, all of whom have a platform and an e-mail list, and they told their list and those people told other people," explains Arielle Ford.

Those e-mails created instant interest—and at $4.95 per download, it was easy for these people to check out the DVD and then tell their friends about it. Which is exactly how I heard about *The Secret*. An otherwise secular and very pragmatic friend in Los Angeles told me I had to check out the DVD online, because "it makes you feel like you're in control and there are possibilities." I asked him how he had heard about it. "My therapist mentioned it, then a friend from the gym, and then someone from AA." Call it viral marketing or word of mouth, it works. No expensive advertising necessary.

The group of filmmakers working in the same subject area also helped spread the word. *Bleep* producer Betsy Chasse describes the community as a brotherhood of folks who have a tradition of helping each other out because they all share the same mission—to enlighten and educate the world. "We have a pact with each other that we will always support each other because we realize we are on the same path. *The Celestine Prophecy, Conversations with God, The Bleep*—each has a newsletter that reaches hundreds of thousands of people, and we support each other's work in those bulletins. So when *The Secret* came out, we figured it was another one of our siblings and we opened our network to them before the movie was well-known, and I think that made a huge difference. But they won't acknowledge that it helped them significantly. We did a huge story in our newsletters and others did too."

Unfortunately, Chasse says, *The Secret* producers refused to do the same thing when other filmmakers released their own topic-related movies. They did nothing about *The Peaceful Warrior* (a March 2007 movie based on Dan Millman's bestselling autobiographical novel *Way of the Peaceful Warrior*), and nothing when *Down the Rabbit Hole* (Chasse's *Bleep* follow-up theatrical film) came out on DVD, according to the producer. "We were surprised by that and thought it [the producers' disinterest] was odd," she recalls.

Ultimately, though, the Hickses, the participants in the movie, and those who work in the same realm all benefit by the incredible exposure *The Secret* has given to the law of attraction and metaphysics. I went to a two-hour talk hosted by John Demartini at EastWest Yoga in New York, and when Demartini asked the audience how many came because they had seen him in *The Secret,* 90 percent of the people in the room raised their hands. Demartini readily admits that *The Secret* opened doors for him, by introducing the already very busy and successful speaker to a new audience unfamiliar with his ideas.

Betsy Chasse describes being in a bookstore in the Pacific Northwest, where she lives, when a young woman walked in who had seen *The Secret.* "She asked the manager for something more in-depth, and the proprietor recommended *The Bleep,* so that kind of thing will happen," she says, "but *The Bleep* has always been a steady seller, and I also hope that people realize that it's about more than simply getting rich." When *What the Bleep* was released on DVD in 2004 it was on Amazon's Top 10 list, says Chasse, and has maintained a position in the Top 100 since then. (On the day I checked Amazon it was 136, still very high for a small-release film that's now more than four years old.)

Web sites of those experts featured in *The Secret,* and even speakers and life coaches who have nothing to do with it, use *The*

Secret as a catchphrase and a platform to entice those who are searching for more information. Topic-related books, including the one you're reading, are in the works or have already been published. Atria Books signed up a book and companion video called *Notes from the Universe* by Mike Dooley, who is featured in *The Secret;* DVD participants James Ray and Lisa Nichols have new books in the works as well.

The Buzz

After the DVD reached its core audience, a more general buzz started to build and the media took notice. For example, it captured the attention of *Larry King Live* executive producer Wendy Walker Whitworth, and the talk-show elder statesman did a two-part story on the DVD and its message. Part 1 was shown on November 1, 2006, and featured DVD participants and law of attraction experts, including success coach Bob Proctor, life coach John Assaraf, inspirational speaker John Demartini, the Reverend Michael Beckwith, and spiritual medium JZ Knight (nee Judith Darlene Hampton), who was born in Roswell, New Mexico, and now channels Ramtha. Part 2 was shown on November 16, 2006, this time featuring success coach James Ray, Jack Canfield of *Chicken Soup* fame, marketing expert Joe Vitale, psychologist George Pratt, and therapist and social worker Jayne Payne.

A small, beautifully produced companion book, essentially a transcript of the DVD with some original material provided by Byrne, was quickly published on November 28, 2006. The book's smallish trim size and ancient-looking cover, adorned with an embossed image of a wax seal, makes it look like it contains special information. On Friday, December 1, Ellen DeGeneres broadcast a segment of *The Secret* on her popular daytime talk show, which featured two of the participants, Bob Proctor and John Assaraf.

Reporters picked up on the phenomenon—which in turn created even more discussion, curiosity, and Internet chatter, along with outrage, jealousy, and jokes. On January 27, 2007, *The Wall Street Journal* was the first national newspaper to pick up on the story. Reporter Camille Ricketts and her colleagues even coined a new term for the genre of DVDs and other media created to uplift and inspire: enlightainment. "We had a roundtable discussion about it in my cubicle," she says. "It was born in the office after a bunch of us threw around a few other alternatives." After Googling the term to see that it wasn't already out there, she went with it in her story.

Ricketts was personally intrigued by the idea of writing about *The Secret.* "I pitched it from a personal place. I watched it in my own life. My mom had sent *The Secret* to me; she has been a fan of this form of thinking for years. I grew up listening to Williamson and Hay," she explains, recalling both the 1990s L.A.-based spiritual superstar, now XM Radio host of *Oprah & Friends* Marianne Williamson, and Louise Hay, the prolific self-help author and founder of Hay House publishers. "I was primed to embrace *The Secret,* and then I saw both book and movie were top sellers on Amazon, so it made sense to cover it."

On February 8, 2007, Oprah devoted an entire show to the book, and then again the following week. The Oprah effect took over. "It's hard to know if a book taps into a certain zeitgeist or creates one," says Sara Nelson, editor of the trade magazine *Publishers Weekly.* "But in the case of *The Secret,* I think a good portion of its mass success is the fact that Oprah spent two entire shows talking about it. That is extremely powerful." Nelson says it is hard to predict how long the book will sell, but the fact that the publisher went back to press for 2 million copies certainly means it will be one of the bestselling books of the year, at least until the new Harry Potter comes along. "Remember, M. Scott Peck's *The Road Less Traveled* was on the list for many years," she says, referring to another popular self-help book written in 1978, at the dawn of the Me Generation.

Allen Salkin says the reason he was first attracted to the idea of writing his February 25, 2007, *Times* piece was because he knew several friends who were going to law of attraction meetings. "A lot of people were talking about the movie. There was something going on, and it was gaining momentum, you could sense it. As a reporter you want to figure out what is going on and why people are so interested in a particular idea. And Rhonda brilliantly managed to convey a sense that there was something mysterious and hidden by the powers that be."

A somewhat less flattering piece about *The Secret* appeared in *Newsweek* on March 5, 2007, "Decoding the Secret," in which senior editor Jerry Adler takes a much dimmer view of the subject matter and its acquisition-focused message. And on March 5, 2007, Peter Berkinhead published a particularly scathing essay, "Oprah's Ugly Secret," in the online magazine *Salon,* attacking the talk-show diva in particular for championing what he sees as a dangerous, materialistic, blame-the-victim concept. In defense of Oprah, I think this was an overreaction and a misreading of her passion for *The Secret.*

Critical Mass

"A lot of reporters since the *Journal* story appeared have pointed out the weakness in *The Secret,*" admits Ricketts. Critics range from longtime practitioners who are disappointed because of its oversimplification to skeptics who charge that the idea is a fantasy that has no basis in reality or science, least of all quantum physics, as believers claim. "I really think that people are so staggered by its success that they want to try to poke holes in it. But I do think it has a place in the self-help canon. The backlash trend is coming from people who are resentful that it is making money and think it is a scam because it is profitable," says Ricketts.

If *The Secret* opens a door and creates an opening for other, less materialistic voices, as a way to improve relationships, that can be a real strength, according to Ricketts. "The get-rich aspect is how you attract a broad audience, but the people who watch it for that do get a dose of the other side."

"Rhonda delivered what she could understand—I think she is actually a detriment to the law of attraction because she is stuck in the 101 version," says Arielle Ford. "But on the other hand, bless her heart, because she has opened up a whole new group of people to the idea."

Chasse argues that because *The Secret* got such a great reception in the beginning, Byrne may not have been ready for what many believe is the predictable onslaught of criticism that often follows, when journalists and others, including envious authors and onlookers, start their scrutiny. After all, her previous programs had never reached such a huge, observant, and opinionated audience. Chasse continues, "She is afraid now," referring to the fact that Byrne retreated from the press and stopped granting interviews. "We were thrown into the fire from the beginning [when *What the Bleep* was released], and faced vicious attacks from the get-go, so we had to be on top of our game because we knew we would get attacked. We knew everything we said would be twisted, and we did the best we could and did our homework and prepared to reply to tough questions."

Two questions in particular emerged again and again. One surrounds Byrne's assertion in the book that people are fat because they think fat, and not because of what they eat. Instead, she recommends that those wanting to lose weight can achieve their goals by not associating or even looking at overweight people, and by having positive thoughts while eating. Don't hesitate to enjoy a Big Mac and fries if the spirit moves you. "She takes it too far with weight," says John Gray. "There is legitimate criticism of that idea. When people eat bad food, they should feel bad. Another version of her weight-loss line of thinking is that if you shoot someone, have a positive thought in your head while you are doing it, so it won't be a bad thing. Obviously it is. And putting bad food in your body is like shooting yourself."

Another idea that raised the ire of many is that you create your own reality and are, in effect, responsible for everything that happens to you, from genetic disease to genocide. What follows from that is the extremely troubling idea that the Jews created the Holocaust and the Rwandans conjured up their own slaughter. In one interview Byrne made the mistake of intimating that this last idea was true. Jerry Adler writes in *Newsweek* that Byrne responded to a question about the Rwandan massacre by saying that people who live in fear and feel powerless unconsciously and innocently attract such events. It's not that simple, as you see in Chapter 3.

Many believers think the book didn't go far enough and some details about how and why to use the law of attraction were left by the wayside. "There is nothing wrong with manifesting a bicycle," says Laura Smith, director of programming for Lime Radio, a health and wellness multimedia brand, referring to a scene in the DVD that shows a little boy pining after, and then receiving, a shiny red two-wheeler. "It is not simply about getting what you want. And you certainly shouldn't do it, for example, by taking it away from someone else."

Still Smith, like everyone who I spoke to in the DVD, is pleased that *The Secret*'s message is reaching people and prompting them to think more deeply about their lives. "I am grateful that people who may have lost the concept that life is good and happiness isn't just for 'other people' but for them too, have found *The Secret,*" she said, echoing what many of her colleagues told me.

Besides, criticism isn't such a bad thing for the book. The fact that there is a pro-and-con discussion going on in newspapers, in other books (like this one), and on the Internet is an increasingly common and sought-after feature of the promotion of media products. Believers see it as positive because people unfamiliar with the idea are now talking about it. It gives detractors a chance to release their cynicism at the entire New Thought movement. And it's good for the marketplace. Discussion keeps books and DVDs such as *The Secret* alive and selling. It's what Massachusetts Institute of Technology professor Henry Jenkins calls "convergence culture." Jenkins, the director of the Comparative Media Studies Program at MIT, writes in his book *Convergence Culture,* "Because there is more information on any given topic than anyone can store in their head, there is an added incentive for us to talk among ourselves about the media we consume. This conversation creates buzz that is increasingly valued by the media industry." In other words, there's no such thing as bad publicity!

Secret communities, both pro and con, have popped up in cyberspace—to analyze it, share experiences with it, and meet like-minded people all over the world. "We have a consumer culture that no longer reduces the recipients to passive consumers," says John Belton, a professor of film and cultural studies at Rutgers

University. "We not only need to tell a story; we need an explanation for it. This movie is providing a platform for others to tell stories, and among them is the story of why this movie or book in particular is so privileged over other storytelling alternatives."

And the cycle of media creating people who create media continues, present company included.

· 2 ·

The Culture of Hope

THE MEGA-SUCCESS OF *The Secret* isn't simply the result of a great promotional campaign. For anything to sustain broad public curiosity for any length of time, whether it's a book, a DVD, or a frozen-food product, it has to have an ingredient that draws people to it. And of course, timing is everything. The combination of six influences, in varying degrees, created the firestorm of interest in both the DVD and the book. The first five can be used as a marketing playbook for anyone wanting to reach a broad-spectrum audience with a self-enhancement product (the last is for believers only).

1. Americans want to be happy.
2. The time is ripe.
3. Baby boomers are searching for new meaning in life.
4. A younger, more self-obsessed generation wants to find that meaning now, and faster.

5. Technology has opened up new avenues of access to information.
6. Rhonda Byrne used the law of attraction to manifest its success.

Hope Springs Eternal—At Least in America

The Secret is part of the happiness movement, which has been around in one form or another since the earliest days of America. Life, liberty, and the pursuit of happiness—Americans consider having a glad heart a birthright, and search for it however and wherever they can. According to the Pew Research Center, only 34 percent of us feel "very happy," most of us—50 percent—are "pretty happy" (meaning we could be happier), and the rest are "not too happy." As a result, the self-help industry rakes in over $9.5 *billion* a year, according to Marketdata Enterprises, a Florida-based research firm. And the company says that one of the two biggest areas of growth is in personal coaching. (The other is infomercials.)

The Secret's themes of redemption and self-improvement are "universally of interest," says *Publishers Weekly*'s Sara Nelson. "It is the power of positive thinking writ large and made easier because, as presented, it is not something you have to do for life. You can do it for twenty minutes and get a BMW. It's the self-improvement culture on speed."

Drugs are also a popular means to the happy ending. The January 2007 professional publication *Lawyers and Settlements* (their slogan is the law of attraction–friendly "Imagine Winning") reported that the U.S. market for antidepressants accounted for 66 percent of the entire global market, compared to 23 percent in Europe, and 11 percent for the rest of world (mostly in Japan).

Since the class of drugs that includes Prozac and Paxil became available in the 1980s, the market has exploded. According to the journal, in 1985 sales of antidepressants in the United States totaled about $240 million, but from September 2003 to August 2004, sales skyrocketed to $11.2 billion.

Of course, pharmacology can only do so much, and many people seek other avenues to find joy. "Happiness 101" is a popular course on college campuses, including Harvard, where Professor Tal Ben-Shahar's standing-room-only class covers topics such as gratitude, goal-setting, relationships, self-esteem, love, and the mind-body connection. Sounds just like *The Secret*! Over at the University of Pennsylvania, Martin Seligman delves deeply into happiness, developing the discipline that Ben-Shahar teaches, called positive psychology. Seligman's research shows that it is possible to *learn* how to feel more satisfied, be more engaged with life, find more meaning in everyday living, have higher hopes, and even laugh more, regardless of circumstances. (More on the mechanics of this in Chapter 3.)

John Suler, a psychology professor at Rider University who teaches the psychology of religion, among other topics, says the positive psychology movement can be traced back to such people as Norman Vincent Peale and his books *The Art of Living* (1937), *Confident Living* (1948), and *The Power of Positive Thinking* (1952).

Yet happiness pundits were dispensing advice well before 1937. A history of the self-help movement is beyond the scope of this book, but there seem to be three key lines of thinking, dating back to the eighteenth and nineteenth centuries, that have influenced modern-day self-help literature: selfless love; changing the way you behave for practical and personal growth; and positive thinking. The influence can be seen in a whole variety of bestselling contemporary books, from twelve-step programs, to Stephen R. Covey's *The 7 Habits of Highly Effective People* (1989), to Marianne Williamson's *A Return to Love* (1996; based on the Christian-focused *A Course in Miracles*), to *The Purpose Driven Life* (2002) by Baptist preacher Rick Warren, to, of course, *The Secret*. Centuries ago, early settlers and struggling pioneers found the New Testament view that a poverty-filled life that was rich in selfless meaning served them well. It made them feel their sacrifices and reduced circumstances were worth enduring because they had a higher purpose, and their reward would come later. In 1770, John Woolman, a Quaker most known for his tireless work against slavery, wrote an essay called "Considerations on the True Harmony of Mankind, and How It Is to Be Maintained." His take on the path to bliss focused on self-sacrifice.

> I have here beheld, how the Desire to provide Wealth, and to uphold a delicate Life, hath grievously entangled many, and been like Snares to their Offspring; and tho' some have been affected with a Sense of their Difficulties . . . where Ways of Living take place, which tend to Oppression, and in the Pursuit of Wealth, People do that to others which they know would not be acceptable to themselves, either in exercising an absolute Power over them, or otherwise laying on them unequitable Burdens. . . . Thus the Harmony of Society is broken, and from hence Commotions and Wars do frequently arise in the World.

About the same time that Woolman's book was published, Benjamin Franklin was working on his autobiography, finishing it in 1788 (it is available for free on the Internet at www .earlyamerica.com/lives/franklin). Franklin has a different take on the road to fulfillment, and it is a view that has won him the title of founding father of America's self-help movement.

Franklin describes thirteen virtues in his autobiography that, once mastered, would earn individuals the joy they desired: temperance, silence, order, resolution, frugality, industry, sincerity, justice, moderation, cleanliness, tranquillity, chastity, and humility.

Franklin, determined to make these virtues habits by consciously practicing them, tracked his progress in the eighteenth-century version of a BlackBerry, a daily calendar that allowed him to check off each time he was successful and give himself a black mark when he wasn't. Frugality and industry, he noted, freed him from remaining debt, produced affluence and independence, and made it easier for him to practice sincerity and justice. Practice makes perfect, and money can buy happiness, if not integrity. It is possible to say here that Franklin used the law of attraction, actively drawing in his virtues by purposefully thinking about those qualities and practicing them. By noticing the bad, however, it is possible he could have attracted the negatives as well. For example, Franklin biographers say he had difficulty achieving a constant state of humility.

Written affirmations was another device Franklin used to promote the virtues he so wanted to perfect. He wrote that he was "convinc'd that truth, sincerity, and integrity in dealings between man and man were of the utmost importance to the felicity of life; and I *formed written resolutions* to practice them ever while I lived." (Italics are mine.)

An affirmation is a statement worded to reprogram the mind with a very specific and positive thought, either material or spiritual. It is a fundamental tool for many self-help and spiritual systems, among them the law of attraction. Law of attraction proponents say it is necessary to write down what you want *as if it already exists* and read the statements daily. (This technique also has links to cognitive therapy, which I will discuss in Chapter 3.) By reading the statement daily, the idea is that it will come to fruition—bringing you closer to meaningful happiness. *The Secret* references the expression "Ask, believe, receive" as steps to attaining your desires. "Name it and claim it" is another popular version of this idea—and its source is biblical (Byrne cites Matthew 21:22 and Mark 11:24).

> And in that day ye shall ask me nothing. Verily, verily, I say unto you, Whatsoever ye shall ask the Father in my name, he will give it you. Hitherto have ye asked nothing in my name: ask, and ye shall receive, that your joy may be full.
>
> JOHN 16:23–24

> And whatsoever ye shall ask in my name, that will I do, that the Father may be glorified in the Son. If ye shall ask any thing in my name, I will do it.
>
> JOHN 14:13–14

> If ye abide in me, and my words abide in you, ye shall ask what ye will, and it shall be done unto you.
>
> JOHN 15:7

The difference between what Franklin was writing, and what the modern law of attraction practitioner might write today is pure content. While Franklin wrote affirmations to help him achieve honesty, ethics, and diligence, a person now is more likely to make declarations like "I am the president of a large company" or "I have all the money I need."

After Franklin, the most influential person in terms of the happiness and self-help movement may be William James, the brother of the novelist Henry James. I radically summarize his work here only to show the clear links between his beliefs and the tradition from which *The Secret* flowed, but for those of you interested, it is well worth reading more about James, including his books.

William James was a Harvard-educated doctor and teacher who at one point during his education suffered a mental breakdown and later credited his religious beliefs (he was a Christian) for his recovery. James was a prolific writer, not of novels, but of nonfiction books, mainly about psychology and religion. *The Principles of Psychology* took twelve years to write; it was completed in 1890 and was considered for many years the seminal book on the subject.

The Will to Believe (1896) and *The Varieties of Religious Experience* (1902) address the psychological reasons people choose and accept religious doctrines. In *Varieties,* James breaks religious beliefs into two categories: those of healthy-minded people and those of sick souls. Healthy-minded believers are optimistic people who willingly exclude evil from their awareness. *They are positive thinkers.* (This idea reminds me of Aldous Huxley's futuristic 1932 novel *Brave New World,* in which the Savage character tells the Controller: "Getting rid of everything unpleasant instead of learning to put up with it. . . . You just abolish the slings and arrows. It's too easy.") The sick soul, said James, cannot help but see evil in life and the result is an unhappy life—*they are negative thinkers.*

People who feel empty and "incomplete" (i.e., unhappy), James wrote, generally seek ways to progress toward a positive ideal. Efforts to improve are stalled by the person's own voluntary efforts, and, says James, it is necessary for the individual to surrender to himself in order to continue the transformation. The religious solution to this problem would be to fill yourself up by submitting to God or, in the case of Christians, Jesus Christ. The AA solution is contained in steps 2 and 3:

2. [We] came to believe that a Power greater than ourselves could restore us to sanity.

3. [We] made a decision to turn our will and our lives over to the care of God as we understood Him.

The Secret puts forward similar ideas but implies that the power that is greater than ourselves (our ego, actually) is our self or mind. It offers a more inner-directed solution: banish bad thoughts and replace them with good.

James was also interested in dual realities and noetics, or "mental science." He experimented with the sedative chloral hydrate, as well as with amyl nitrite and nitrous oxide, as a way to experience "mystical states." Speculating that the subconscious self could be a portal to a supernatural region, James defined this realm as the power or energy many people can most easily grasp as God. Similarly, the ideological foundation of metaphysical thought, including that expressed in *The Secret,* is the sense that our consciousness (and in some cases, our unconscious thought) creates our reality.

The Times, They Are A-Changin'

Aside from our general predisposition to seek information that helps increase our self-worth, there is a strong sense among all the people I interviewed that acceptance of *The Secret*'s message has been brewing in the culture for a while. An unpopular war and perceived economic problems have created an environment that opens people to seek alternative answers to address their unease with the world. "People want a solution; there is a sense that people are not living the life they want and of not having control. The discontent is odd because supposedly statistically we are in a good place," says One Spirit Book Club's Kristine Pidkameny. So when a simple way out comes along, it hits a nerve.

Ideas "tend to work in cycles and balances in the world, including human culture and the human psyche. When things get bad and negative, the idea of thinking positive arises. Our media seems to love reporting catastrophic events and scandals, so the development of grassroots positive thinking might be an antidote to that," according to Rider University professor John Suler.

"One thing going on in our culture at the moment, and what interests me, is that we find ourselves in a very ticky-tacky world," says physicist Fred Alan Wolf, who appears in both *The Secret* and *What the Bleep,* referencing Malvina Reynolds's classic folk song "Little Boxes," which basically describes how everyone is living in the same "ticky-tacky" house, and wearing the same clothes, and eating the same food (lyrics are available at ingeb.org/songs/littlebo.html).

"Success in America is to be like everyone else, but for many people that's not enough, and they increasingly wonder, What does it mean to be successful, what is the real measure? The way we work makes people more depressed, so we are looking for an answer to the question, Is there more?" says Wolf. "There is a wonderful scene in *Scarface* that exemplifies this. Al Pacino is relaxing in a bubble bath in his mansion and he looks around and asks, 'Is this all there is?'"

Americans are also getting smarter, and less willing to accept the word of authority, says Wolf, despite cries to the contrary. "Fifty years ago, when our president came out and said A, B, and C, we would believe him. But now when a politician says something, we think maybe it is actually X, Y, and Z." The same mistrust and curiosity that make us question our leaders also cause us to look into what it means to be alive and question conventional scientific explanations. "There will always be Neanderthals—religious rightists and extreme leftists roaming the planet along with atheists," says Wolf, but most people are in the middle and the pat answers aren't enough for them anymore. No one idea meets the needs of the majority. Indeed, *The Secret* is on the bestseller list right alongside *The God Delusion* by Richard Dawkins, a book that strives to prove not that God is dead but that He never existed in the first place.

Publishers Weekly's Sara Nelson also thinks *The Secret*'s religious tone appeals to a certain segment of today's reading population, who are continuously on the hunt for a meaning and a message. "It comes on the heels of *The Purpose Driven Life,*" says Nelson, the widely successful book by Southern Baptist preacher Rick Warren, who heads up the enormous southern California Saddleback Church. But *The Secret* is not by a celebrity preacher telling you how to live your life. "It is not evangelical, it is by regular people telling you how to [create a faith] yourself, and make it your own," according to Nelson. It is a trend she thinks will continue the long history of books telling us how to be better, more successful people. "What's fashionable right now in the movement is the DIY [do-it-yourself] aspect," says Nelson.

Inspirational speaker and coach John Demartini often works with hospital patients and medical professionals, and he sees the idea showing up in the health-care system as well. "The door is opened to people taking some accountability for their own welfare and health. People are receptive to the idea that they can empower their lives."

Metaphysical marketing professional Arielle Ford agrees. "Think about it. It is very empowering [in an unpredictable world] to believe that you can have control over your life, that you can have an intention and open yourself up to it. For those of us in the New Thought world this is not new, but for a lot of people it is, and they think, 'Wow! Look what all these famous people did. It is amazing.'" What naturally follows is the thought, Why not me too?

Boom!

Baby boomers are fueling a lot of the recent fervor for do-it-yourself wisdom, the women in particular. Things are changing for these ladies, and they need help figuring out how to bring meaning and enjoyment to the next thirty or forty years. One Spirit's Kristine Pidkameny says her core audience, who embraced *The Secret,* is "primarily boomer women who are drawn to our offerings when they reach those middle years; it is a passage of contemplation, and a lot of our books address midlife issues to help them through the transition."

Marketdata's research director, John LaRosa, noted in a press statement that there is no shortage of demand for products and programs that allow Americans, especially affluent female baby boomers, to make more money, lose weight, improve relationships and business skills, cope with stress, or obtain a quick dose of motivation—all things knowledge and practice of *The Secret* promises.

As a baby boomer I understand the appeal of a system that helps create second chances and aids reinvention. Many of us in our forties and fifties view working in the same office until we retire as damned unappealing. Still, most of us will work past the age of sixty-five, out of both desire and necessity. According to a comprehensive spring 2007 study of the changing habits of boomer women, *Baby Boomer Women: Secure Futures or Not?* edited by Paul Hodge, director of the Harvard Generations Policy

Program and a research fellow at the John F. Kennedy School of Government, women want to be productive into our sixties and beyond because the prospect of a thirty-year vacation doesn't hold much appeal. Plus, we are going to need the money. The majority of us don't have enough in our retirement accounts to pay for the rest of our lives. Anything that can help improve the second stage of our personal or business lives holds a great deal of allure.

The Marketdata research also noted a growing trend of baby boomers using the help of "gurus" as opposed to, or in conjunction with, more traditional forms of help like therapists and business consultants. This interest has allowed a handful of self-help celebrities like Tony Robbins, Deepak Chopra, and Suze Orman to leverage their names to build multimedia, multiplatform empires, says LaRosa. And now we can add Rhonda Byrne to the list.

Generation Z

It seems *The Secret* has another less obvious audience: young people, including many guys, who are attracted by the materialistic aspect of the book and the DVD's promise. Arielle Ford was surprised to see so many young men in Wall Street suits at a free event held recently by life coach James Ray, one of *The Secret* experts. "It's unusual to see people like that at such occasions, but the room was bursting at the seams with them, so I started asking a couple why they were there," she says. They had seen *The Secret* and wanted to know more. "On one level it is great for those who are willing to take the next steps, and learn more or attend a workshop, but the opportunity to make money is what motivated them to attend."

Bleep coproducer Betsy Chasse says sales on her site for Wallace Wattles's *The Science of Getting Rich* spiked dramatically after *The Secret* became a hit. "Our *Bleep* store has become a haven for people who want the cutting edge in spirituality and science, and that's what our typical audience is looking for. So we were amused that's where the mainstream consciousness is. Seventy percent of those people who try it are going to fail"—although, notes Chasse, it may not be such a bad thing if the population got rich because they could then move on. "We are all worried about surviving, and to be enlightened you have to get over survival worries. Maybe that's a good thing about *The Secret*—ultimately if humanity becomes enlightened they can move beyond the material stuff."

Young people's interest makes sense from another perspective—the newest generation of adults often embraces ideas of previous generations simply because the ideas are new to them. "Many people in their twenties have approached me with an interest in *The Secret*," says John Gray, author of *Men Are from Mars, Women Are from Venus*. "It's a new awakening for them." Pidkameny sees the same thing in her club: "Younger people in their twenties are buying it because they want to know the secret of how to get where they want to go quicker."

There's also a dark side to young people's interest in *The Secret*. Generation Me, the group in their twenties and thirties, are more self-interested than previous generations, according to Jean Twenge, psychology professor at San Diego State University and author of *Generation Me: Why Today's Young Americans Are More Confident, Assertive, Entitled—and More Miserable Than Ever Before*. She says this group has grown up with the idea that self-esteem is more important than achievement. Twenge undertook the largest study ever to look at generational changes in narcissism, which was conducted by a team of psychologists from a variety of universities.

"Far from being civically oriented, young people born after 1982 are the most narcissistic generation in recent history," Twenge argues. She does not find it surprising that many of them would find the think-your-way-to-fame concept appealing. "The children of baby boomers have learned from their parents that they can be whatever they want to be, they have learned that if you believe in yourself anything is possible. What is different about this is that previous generations recognized hard work was also necessary to make it, and now we question that." The result is that young people believe they can make anything happen without effort. The focus on the self is also different from classic types of individualism (think Ayn Rand), which included a lot of ambition, creativity, and hard work.

Yet there are hardworking young people who come to the law of attraction because it shows them possibilities they didn't realize could be part of their experience. John Gray told me about his twenty-two-year-old mechanic who generally doesn't read many books. "He told me he saw *The Secret* and was blown out of his mind by it. He had never heard of the information in it, and it made him feel very empowered. Once he saw the movie he had to have the book too."

In this case, Gray thinks that for people who have never been exposed to the idea that you really can control your destiny, that decisions are yours to make, not to be forced upon you, is especially potent. "It was wonderful for this young guy to see these mentors and then see that it could be applied to his own life." For cynics who think a working-class young guy could be disappointed by the book's promise (whatever you want is yours for the asking), Gray counters by saying that the perspective naysayers have on positive thinking is misdirected.

"Anyone who has created anything started with a positive thought—it takes hard work, yes, but the effort gets started with an optimistic perspective. People who have had role models or someone who has supported them take that attitude for granted. For those who do not operate from that context, like my mechanic friend, who may not have had that in their lives, this can be the door opening."

John Demartini points out that the message is not limited to the material. Rather, people come to it for different reasons, based on what is highest within their personal value system— that's what they see. "If it's money, so be it. For others it could be family or relationships. Right now with the economy, and the fact that we have a negative savings system, there is a void in that area. I look at the book and don't see it because finances are not my highest value."

The Spirit in the Machine: Technology

Metaphysical thinking was once confined to a smallish group of people who purposefully sought out alternative solutions. But the Web has changed everything. Inspirational speaker and life coach John Demartini attributes the growing mainstream interest in the law of attraction and its metaphysical relatives (mysticism, Taoism) to the easy availability of ideas on the Internet. "We have access to a wide dissemination of information that a decade ago we could not have achieved because the technology wasn't there. We can create information in a format that appeals to the eye and grabs the attention of people," which, he says, *The Secret* does brilliantly.

Not only was it first easily and cheaply accessible as an Internet download, but it speaks in "televisionese," a language that everyone understands. *What the Bleep,* a film made for theatrical release, uses shifting narrative perspectives, and many other filmic devices that are commonly employed in experimental film (think Stan Brakhage and Luis Buñuel). *The Secret* uses the language of infomercials, with talking heads and pretty graphics, to make its points easily digestible for the greatest number of people.

Internet access and the offshoots of Web-based *Secret* discussion groups and message boards indicate a shift in how we communicate spiritual and religious ideas. "All of these things will result in new kinds of spiritual communications, expressions, and communities," says psychologist John Suler. "I don't think the Internet will replace old forms of spiritual communication. It will be a supplement and enhancement. Geographic distance poses no problem. People can communicate in real or delayed time frames. Everyone can have their own voice and express themselves with words, images, and music. People who could never meet before can now meet." And round and round *The Secret* goes.

"I think what came before *The Secret* also ripened the climate of curiosity and acceptance in the mainstream of its ideas," says Kristine Pidkameny, pointing to the films *What the Bleep* and *Down the Rabbit Hole.* Both these films grabbed the attention of people via word of mouth on the Internet. "The interest now [in metaphysics] isn't so much left of center, which I think it frequently is normally. I watched the word of mouth for *What the Bleep* grow and it started crossing over to the general public."

Pidkameny points to one feature of *What the Bleep* that flowed into the mainstream in part via Internet chat rooms and bloggers. "That book that blew out from the movie was Dr. Masaru Emoto's *The Hidden Messages in Water.*" Emoto conducted a series of experiments with water crystals. He exposed water to positive messages, writing words such as "love," "kindness," "joy," and "hope" on paper and taping them to water containers so the liquid could "see" them. Another group of water containers were exposed to negative words and thoughts. Upon freezing, the water that was exposed to positive vibes formed beautiful snowflake-like crystals, whereas the water exposed to negative vibes formed unattractive shapes. Emoto has suffered a backlash from many people, scientists included, who say his experiment was not scientific, and challenge him to conduct more rigorous trials to prove his assertions, offers which he has so far declined. "The criticism did not seem to affect book sales," says Pidkameny.

As an example of how quickly information can be obtained through media and cyberspace, and then morphed into new enterprises and ideas, take one Dushan Zaric, owner and bartender at a bar in Greenwich Village, New York, called Employees Only. According to a story in the March 4, 2007, *New York Times* Sunday Style section, the bartender fashioned a cocktail experiment based on Emoto's waterworks. Five bartenders all made the same daiquiri with exactly the same ingredients. Every time a happy and confident bartender made the drink, customers and staff said it tasted better than when a depressed or anxiety-ridden bartender made it. Bloggers and members of foodie chat rooms continue to discuss the innkeeper's experiment online. "That's really diluting the message," notes MIT media professor Henry Jenkins.

Rhonda Byrne Is a Metaphysician

The real secret behind *The Secret* could very well be Rhonda Byrne herself. "The success is a perfect example of Rhonda manifesting her vision," says John Gray. "What's unusual is that she has manifested her dream, which was to tell people how to manifest *their* dreams." Gray qualifies this by pointing out that Byrne's well-honed professional and creative abilities helped. "Manifesting your dreams is possible, but you need preparation, talent, and skills. Those are the first things necessary." Enforced reinvention was part of it too. Byrne had entered what she described as a down period of her life, and bottomed out. "Pain, hurt, exclusion—the great thinkers and creators all experienced these things. Then, like Rhonda, they rose up again," explains Gray, who says that the value of the negative is an aspect of the law of attraction that is missing from the book. Law of attraction teachers Jerry and Esther Hicks have pointed to this reasoning too, saying in the letter they wrote to friends that they admire Byrne's ability to stay in "alignment" with her manifestation efforts.

So obviously this begs the question, does the law of attraction really work?

· 3 ·

Does It Work?

THE CREDIBLE ASPECTS of the law of attraction, and there are several, are found within a group of interrelated psychological theories that include the placebo effect; mindfulness theory; cognitive therapy; and its newer cousin, positive psychology. Call it the science of happiness or optimism studies—it has merit. Those who face reality, exercise free will by making decisions consciously and accepting responsibility for them, reserve judgment, and believe in themselves create happier, richer lives than those who can't or don't. Life is full of chance and risk, and it's safe to say that those of us who are willing to go out on a limb sometimes fall, but more often than not, we can achieve more greatness than those who stay safely tucked into the crotch of the tree.

True followers of the law of attraction, however, don't need academic proof. When you have unwavering confidence in a concept or person, science and empirical reasoning—even actual experience—are unnecessary. For people who have no religious background, faith can be a difficult concept to swallow or understand. Even in "secular religions," which the law of attraction is most certainly part of, no amount of evidence to the contrary will change the believer's mind. You can actually start and end the discussion about the efficacy of the law of attraction right there: "It is so because I believe it to be so."

One of the simplifications in *The Secret* that has aroused controversy is the easy, self-incriminating excuse it gives when people fail to attain their desires. You see, if you don't *really* believe, nothing will happen—so there's always an out when a faith-based believer is faced with a critic. You didn't get the car because you did not *truly* think you deserved it. You still have cancer because *deep down inside* you think you should be sick. I don't know about you, but I have felt sure something was *not* going to happen in my life, and by gum, it happened anyway.

Harvard psychology researcher Ellen Langer says that there is evidence to support the idea that believing that you can bring yourself $1 million can result in the money. But there's a catch and it involves action, something that is not really addressed in *The Secret:* "You may process information differently once you believe. You start to think about finances and money differently, take actions to make money, and will no longer be blind to moneymaking opportunities."

This reminds me of a very successful self-made woman I met recently, who told me that when she was about seventeen she was driving her poor family's old car back from her afterschool job, and it broke down. She had to call her dad to retrieve her and the car, since calling a mechanic was financially out of the question. At that moment, she recalled, "I understood what a drag it was that my car broke down, but I also saw it as a chance to clarify what I wanted out of life. At that moment, I said, 'I will never be poor.' And I'm not." Of course, she consciously chose a path in life that included getting an M.B.A. and a job selling hedge funds—a very direct route to making money.

Rhonda Byrne's manifestation of success for her DVD included certain decisions and actions (outlined in Chapter 1) that resulted in traveling to the United States and meeting the experts and speakers who would participate in her film, and using a distribution system different from her original broadcast plan (Internet download). No matter how many times she had written down and read out loud, "I made a hugely successful film about the law of attraction," if she simply sat in her Sydney home it's fairly certain that nothing would have happened.

In short, "Ask, believe, receive" might be more accurately expressed this way: "Ask, believe, act, and (greatly increase your chances to) receive."

A Fly in the Ointment

Even some believers express concern that *The Secret* simplifies the concept of attraction to such a degree that it is rendered useless, particularly for novices who have no other information about it. "The flaws are obvious," says Arielle Ford, who has been immersed in the metaphysical world for more than twenty-five years. "There will be disappointed people because Rhonda does not spend enough time talking about the need to feel and believe that what you want is already yours. Unless you can do that, you can't have it. Most people find that difficult because they believe they are unworthy, and are filled with dread and shame. They may say, 'I want to be rich,' but they have a loser mentality, and nowhere in *The Secret* is there information about how to embrace your loser-ness."

"I would love to have seen other components in the DVD," says life coach and *Secret* contributor John Demartini. "There are so many things I would have clarified. At the same time I am grateful it went out to a mass market." Demartini's workshops teach that there is a hierarchy of values from which people manifest things in their life. (A popular two-day event is called the Breakthrough Experience.) "If you go after something that is not congruent with your value system, you will keep going back to what's important to you." While Demartini's language can be construed as New Age, it is not without pragmatism. If you are going after something that is not probable, it's not going to happen, he says.

Gail Jones, a Boston-area life coach and author of the book *To Hell and Back . . . Healing Your Way Through Transition,* works mainly with baby boomers going through midlife changes in careers and relationships. Jones says she finds the "belief piece" missing from *The Secret.* Not "belief" in the sense that you believe your positive thought will happen, but that unless you are aware of your inner beliefs and values, you can never really achieve true change or realize your desires. "*The Secret* is too simple. Before you can ask for something, you have to be clear about what you really think about yourself. You have to clear beliefs about yourself that are holding you back (I'm not good enough, etc.) and replace them with new ones (I deserve this, etc.)." Jones says this is almost impossible to do on your own—and necessitates the help of a coach or a therapist.

Ben Johnson, who has degrees in medicine, naturopathic medicine, and osteopathy, participated in *The Secret,* and worries that the DVD's viewers often come away with a "be all and end all" idea that "all we have to do is think, ask, believe, and whatever we want will fall out of the sky. No matter how much positive thought or warm and fuzzy stuff we put out, you cannot discount the rule of three: it takes three times as long, costs three times as much, and requires three times as much energy to get anywhere you want to go. And, you need to find your passion so that your work is productive."

Betsy Chasse says *The Secret* is easy to attack because there is not enough substance in it, but adds, "We do not know half of what the brain can do." Exactly right. Scientists and psychologists have long studied how our thoughts and moods intersect, and there are a significant number of studies that show how an optimistic approach to life has quantifiable psychological, physiological, and biological effects on our health and well-being.

The Belief Response: Placebo Effect and Mindfulness Theory

The word "placebo" derives from the Latin for "I shall please." It refers to a benign treatment, which includes a sugar pill, faux surgery, or a definitive suggestion about the recipient's health that can result in improvement from illness or symptoms, and in some cases, depending on what is believed at the time the placebo is given, worsening of health or symptoms. Belief in the placebo imbues it with medicinal power.

Flashback to the wisdom of the old guys: Our friend William James, the nineteenth-century psychologist, said, "Whilst part of what we perceive comes through our senses from the object before us, another part (perhaps the larger part) always comes . . . out of our own head." And Marcus Aurelius said, "If you are distressed by anything external, the pain is not due to the thing itself, but to your estimate of it; and this you have the power to revoke at any moment."

Howard Brody, director of the Institute for the Medical Humanities at the University of Texas Medical Branch and author of the book *The Placebo Response: How You Can Release the Body's Inner Pharmacy for Better Health,* says that "recent studies continue to show the placebo response is very real and we are getting a better sense of what is at the base of it. In the last five years neuroimaging has been very promising in placebo study, although still exploratory." Neuroimaging is the study of the structure, function, and pharmacology of the brain. It allows scientists to see how information is processed in the brain, and in turn how the brain responds, which includes the ability to direct the healing of ailments. It has broad implications for the diagnosis and treatment of Alzheimer's disease, metabolic illnesses, and general brain and cognitive research.

Brody describes a 2001 study done with patients with Parkinson's disease. Some were given a drug that increased dopamine in the brain and others were given a placebo. The placebo patients had a statistically significant increase in brain production of dopamine. "The same thing happened that would have happened if they had been given the drug," he says. Natural opiate manufacture occurs in pain studies when placebos are used. In studies of depression, you can see an increase of activity in the area of the brain that controls mood, mimicking the brain activity seen in those who take antidepressants.

There are two theories about why placebos are as effective as drugs in some people: expectancy and conditioning. "Expectancy says the patient anticipates getting better, and does," explains Brody. "But how does the brain know what works to make it better? Conditioning theory says that the brain remembers that the body got better in the past, and when you administer a placebo it turns on that memory and opens up the pathway that allows whatever is needed to heal the body."

Yet placebo occurs only in a certain percentage of people.

Many estimates say one-third of placebo patients report effects similar to those who received therapy or drugs. But there has never been a placebo test that has worked in 100 percent of recipients. "Some will have it and some won't, so it is relatively unpredictable," says Brody.

The unpredictability of placebo responses led two Dutch scientists to issue a paper debunking the theory as a fairy tale. The paper appeared in the May 2001 issue of *The New England Journal of Medicine*. Dr. Asbjorn Hrobjartsson and Dr. Peter C. Gotzsche, of the University of Copenhagen and the Nordic Cochran Center, an international organization of medical researchers who review randomized clinical trials, looked at 114 published placebo-and-drug studies involving approximately 7,500 patients with forty different conditions. They found no support for the conventional wisdom that one-third of patients improve when given a dummy pill they believe is real, and no reason to think there is a mind-body connection. However, Brody contends this is a minority view, and new studies on the placebo response continue to show impressive results.

Harvard psychology professor Ellen Langer, author of *Mindfulness: The Power of Mindful Learning* and *Mindful Creativity,* has long done research into the placebo effect, or what she calls mindfulness theory. "Right now the placebo process is silly," she says. "Someone has to lie to you convincingly." She's trying to find a way to circumvent the placebo pill or therapy itself (and the accompanying lie) and find a way for the healing mechanism it triggers to work for more people, on demand.

"The main problem that psychologists have is how to get from the nonmaterial mind to the material body [when desired]," says Langer. "The idea that you can make something happen by thinking about it on the face of it seems outlandish.

Right now there is no reason to believe it, but that is different from 'It must be wrong,'" asserts Langer. "We have examples of how thought results in biological changes. We see a mouse. A mouse is not going to hurt you, but your pulse and your blood pressure go up. Or you eat something, and then someone tells you that the chef peed on it. You might even vomit." So how do we find the chemical or neurological connection between the thought (I think the chef peed in my soup—he did not) and the result (I'm sick for days)?

One of Langer's recent studies goes right to the heart of that issue and to one of the most debated and hotly contested claims in *The Secret*. In the book (but not the DVD) Byrne describes gaining a lot of weight after her daughters were born. She attributed this to reading about and subsequently believing it is common for women to put on the pounds at that time in their lives. She says people gain weight not from eating too much but by thinking that food makes you fat. As long as you do not believe a food will make you fat, she says, you can eat it with no adverse affect.

Byrne recommends believing you are already your perfect weight, and avoiding looking at anyone who is overweight (one wonders what direction she looks in when she appears on shows with a live audience). This reminds me of old superstitions about illness: Don't associate with people who have cancer because you might catch it. Is that what Byrne is saying? Well, in the book she says that you should not discuss a person's illness with them because you're asking for it.

However, Langer found evidence to suggest that thinking thin may actually result in weight loss. When Langer and one of her students studied a group of eighty-four housekeepers working in seven Boston hotels, she found a remarkable result (published in the February 2007 issue of *Psychological Science*). The women ranged in age from eighteen to fifty-five years old.

Housekeepers in four of the hotels were told that their work cleaning fifteen rooms a day was good exercise and met the guidelines for a healthy, active lifestyle. The women working in the remaining three hotels were told nothing.

The housekeepers filled out questionnaires, which showed that the amount of activity they engaged in did not change over the four-week study period. The women in the "healthy lifestyle" group lost an average of two pounds and 0.5 percent of their body fat; they reduced their body-mass index by 0.35 of a point; and their systolic blood pressure (the first number) dropped an average of 10 percent. The women who were told nothing showed no statistically significant changes. While a two-pound weight loss over four weeks isn't dramatic, it is on the low end of doctors' recommendations for healthy weight loss, from one-half to three pounds per week, which is more easily sustained over the long haul.

Think about how much of the time we are oblivious and mindless, advises Langer. Science processes probabilities and they get translated into absolute facts in the culture. "Once you think you know something for sure (for example, housekeeping isn't exercise), you no longer pay attention to it," she says. "As a result of not paying attention we are frequently in error and never in doubt." We can also miss opportunities that can take us where we want to go or allow us to have beneficial experiences.

"Absolute notions, in my view, freeze your mind. Not having absolute notions keeps you attentive and you will see things that you would not otherwise see," says Langer. "When we hear a claim that cannot possibly be true, the question becomes, Let's look at it and make sure. Saying we cannot be sure it is not true is very different from saying something is absolutely true or certainly false. Actively noticing new things without adding a preconceived notion makes you more aware of how little you know, and that process of actively drawing distinctions makes you more lively."

Langer's work is designed to take a look at "absolute" truths or beliefs to see if they can be shifted to find alternative truths. She tells me about the horse and the hotdog. A man wants to get a hotdog for his horse. You might think, Well, the horse won't eat it because horses don't eat meat. Then the man gives the horse a hotdog, and she eats it. Then you have to think, there are factors and circumstances where horses will eat meat after all. It suggests a possibility—it does not mean all horses will eat meat all the time. If your mind-set is stubbornly fixed on the idea that horses do not eat meat, and hotdogs were the only food option available, your horse might starve to death because you won't attempt to feed the poor nag a frank.

Thoughts that result in certain outward projections can also change our circumstances, and if they cannot change *the* world, at least thoughts can change *your* world. Many of us have been on the "perceiving end" of the example Howard Brody relates of recently passing over a job candidate. "We didn't hire the person as a faculty member in part because she did not send out confidence vibes. So while we cannot magically change the world or part the Red Sea, psychological forces can make a causal difference in the way the world works." In this case, the woman's thoughts about her qualifications were manifested in behavioral cues that resulted in rejection.

It's even possible that the woman was qualified, but wasn't feeling so well that day: "The assumptions used to be that I can emotionally feel and I can think and those are two different things. The idea was used as an excuse for gender bias. 'Women are more emotional than men,' and so forth. But it turns out that the two centers in the brain that control emotion and logic are intimately wired together, and you cannot trigger one without making a cross-connect with the other," says Brody.

Curing Powers

Another aspect of *The Secret,* which has been met with anger and skepticism, is the conviction that thinking positively can cure disease—cancer included; this conviction may have occurred because believers have misread the nuances of placebo and positivity theories. The book includes the story of Cathy Goodman, who claims to have cured her cancer by believing she did not have cancer and by watching funny movies. *Secret* contributors I talked to all said they never suggest that people stop traditional therapies. The book's simplification opens gullible and desperate sick people to scams and dangerous behavior. Oprah had to clarify her position during the March 30, 2007, show after a woman had written to her that she had watched her initial program about *The Secret* and shortly afterward found out that she had breast cancer; she was told by three doctors that she needed a mastectomy immediately, but decided instead to think herself well. Oprah tried to talk some sense into the viewer by explaining that *The Secret* does not advocate eliminating conventional forms of medical treatment. It doesn't, but Byrne does write that you will be well if you believe you are perfect.

"I do not recommend people stop taking their cancer meds," says John Demartini, "although there are no doubt spontaneous remissions (they are a statistical rarity), and I do believe our emotions have something to do with them." Dr. Ben Johnson, who, along with Dr. Alex Lloyd, promotes and sells a product called the Healing Codes that Johnson claims eliminate damaging unconscious thoughts *literally* hidden in cells. He says he used the Codes on himself to cure Lou Gehrig's disease. "You have to throw everything you've got at illness," he says. The Healing Codes system, which costs $797, uses Corellian photography and energy from the tips of your fingers to activate the four healing centers in the body in specific sequences. According to Johnson, once the lies are taken out of the memories stored in your cells, health can be yours. The idea that all illness is caused by bad memories in the cells sounds like an extremely mystical use of the term "memory."

Norman Doidge is the author of *The Brain That Changes Itself: Stories of Personal Triumph from the Frontiers of Brain Science* (2007) and a research faculty member at the Columbia University Center for Psychoanalytic Training and Research and the University of Toronto Department of Psychiatry. "I am a big believer in the link between the brain and the body, but these assertions take that link and extend it so far, make it so nonspecific, that it almost becomes meaningless," says Doidge. "What does it mean to say a cell has a bad memory? It is a metaphor derived from our conscious experience or memory, and attributes this complex state to a cell, or cells. Since, of course, we all have bad memories of some sort, we all qualify, presumably, as having bad cell memories too, and therefore get ill. Yet such a nonspecific approach doesn't explain why some people get one illness, and not another. It explains little, and only gains our attention on the basis of the assertion that it cures. But the only way to know if it does cure would be to do some carefully conducted study." There are no empirical, controlled studies of the Healing Codes, although Johnson says he has many testimonials.

Doidge also points out that outbreaks of infectious diseases don't only infect those with "bad cell memories"—everyone succumbs to the epidemic. The problem with blaming bad memories for illness is that one "enters a universe that is not different from the world of primitive and medieval response to illness, where, in the absence of any understanding of the microscopic world, the sick are blamed as being bad, or sinners, or evil, or possessed by something evil."

Far-out alternative treatments notwithstanding, numerous rigorous studies have shown that an optimistic outlook improves a sick person's chances of healing more quickly than a person who is pessimistic. So many, in fact, that the citations alone would fill a book of this size. (I've listed several important studies in the "Further Reading" section at the end of this book.) An oft-cited Harvard research project found that optimism among college students predicted their health thirty-five years later. A group of Ivy League undergraduates were studied during World War II and then followed through their adult lives. Researchers found that the optimistic students had better health in middle age than those who had been pessimistic as students.

Cathy Goodman said she watched comedies as part of her treatment—laughter is the best medicine. It could be, according to David L. Felten, medical research director at the Beaumont Research Institute and William Beaumont Hospitals in Royal Oak, Michigan, coeditor of *Psychoneuroimmunology,* and cofounder and editor of the journal *Brain, Behavior and Immunity.* Dr. Felten says studies show that watching a half-hour humor video stimulates natural killer cells and antitumor defenses. "We have seen it in clinical work and controlled studies; in one, cardiac patients' recurrent heart attacks were decreased by 80 percent when a half-hour of video viewing was included in their daily treatment over those who did not watch humor videos."

In another study, published in 2005, researchers from the Finnish Institute of Occupational Health, National Research and Development Centre for Welfare and Health, Universities of

Helsinki and Turku and University College London examined health changes in 5,007 people who experienced either the death or onset of severe illness in a family member. Their individual pessimism and optimism levels were assessed three years before and after the stressful life event. The researchers found that the number of sick days taken after the major event decreased to the pre-event levels more quickly for people who scored higher on optimism questionnaires than for those who had low optimism scores.

The authors concluded that optimism reduces the risk of health problems and can help people recover after experiencing a serious life-changing event. As for the pessimists, the researchers note that they "frequently distance themselves from emotional events and this coping strategy may be less effective than using active problem-focused coping immediately after an uncontrollable severe event such as death of a family member."

Vanderbilt University psychologist Oakley Ray says that stress affects the brain and can hurt the body at the cellular and molecular level, diminishing a person's health and quality of life. Yet, he's found that maintaining a positive frame of mind can help a person overcome some of the damaging effects of stress, fight disease better, and ultimately delay death.

"Knowing how the brain influences people's health and susceptibility to illness can bring important changes to the health-care system. Understanding how the mind, the endocrine system, the nervous system, and immune system all interact, known as psychoendoneuroimmunology, or PENI, is crucial in helping people conquer the stress in their lives and stay healthy," said Ray. For example, Ray says there are pathogens that can live in equilibrium with us—like tuberculosis—with only a small percentage developing symptoms and exhibiting illness. Those who don't get sick probably have a well-functioning PENI system.

Studies of mortality rates of patients suffering from fatal illnesses such as lung cancer do not see many reversals of health, no matter their attitude. A 2004 Australian study published in the journal *Cancer* found that having an optimistic attitude does not help lung cancer patients live longer. In fact, the researchers found that encouraging an optimistic attitude in these patients could actually be harmful because the effort to be or act happy often represents an additional burden.

The study also found that these patients' optimism decreased over time, even if the patients responded well to treatment—perhaps because of the toxic treatments they received and because of the serious nature of their illness. Researchers noted that these results are not particularly shocking to the oncologists they interviewed. All of them said they see patients with advanced lung cancer begin treatment with a great deal of hope, only to fail as quickly as patients who feel pessimistic about their chances. It seems particularly cruel to blame patients for their progress or lack thereof because they find it difficult to take a glass-half-full approach to their treatment and grave situation.

Optimism is also next to useless when accompanied by denial—and the two should never be confused. Denial can result in people not taking medical steps to fight illness or to even bother taking care of themselves, while realistic optimism helps patients seize control of their care. That's another reason why realistic optimists' survival rates are better than both deniers and depressed realists, who are less likely to care whether they live or die, and behave accordingly.

Another significant, and hopeful, development in the mind-body connection to healing is in the area of guided imagery (GI). *The Secret* would call this visualization—picture what you want to happen and it will. Guided imagery is a deep-relaxation technique that is now widely accepted by traditional health-care professionals. The idea that mental pictures can produce healing sounds pretty out there, but strong evidence suggests there is a connection between what we imagine and how we heal. Many credible controlled studies have shown GI to be effective in reducing recovery time after surgery, making cancer treatment easier to take, lessening anxiety, relieving arthritis, and reducing blood pressure.

For example, Columbia University Medical Center researchers found that heart surgery patients who received GI showed statistically significant physical and psychological improvement compared to patients who passed on the alternative technique and used only conventional treatment. Blue Shield of California studied more than nine hundred hysterectomy patients and discovered that those who listened to a GI tape before surgery saved about $2,000 in treatment costs, mainly due to a reduction in the need for pain meds. The insurer now offers all surgery patients GI tapes to prepare for their procedure.

In GI, a therapist helps patients identify certain relaxing images that they can then use to enter into a state of very deep relaxation (sometimes referred to as an alpha state). Psychologists say GI works for many people because in terms of brain response there is very little difference between thinking about something and experiencing it. The visual cortex is closely intertwined with the automatic nervous system, which controls the pulse and breathing, among other involuntary events. So, for example, when you eat a lemon you salivate; the same thing happens when you think about eating a lemon. Experiencing 9/11 in Manhattan made me very upset—recalling that day does the same thing. My heart races, tears well up, and I feel very sad. Thinking about a funny experience I had with a friend makes me laugh as hard as the day we were together.

GI is not something you can do yourself in one fell swoop. Most practitioners say it takes practice and some training (although listening to a GI tape does help). Most GI therapists say that six or eight sessions with a trained professional are ideal, accompanied by a continued use of tapes (which are generally very inexpensive; many are less than $20).

There is a large body of experimental research that supports the effectiveness of cognitive-therapy techniques in relieving depression, losing weight, solving problems, and becoming a more effective person in general. Cognitive therapy seeks to replace dysfunctional, irrational, negative, untrue, or sabotaging thoughts with more rational, realistic, and positive thoughts. The technique has proven that there is a link between how consciously changing our thoughts can change our behavior. However, Robert L. Leahy, president of the International Association for Cognitive Psychotherapy and professor of clinical psychiatry at the Weill Cornell Medical Center, believes that *Secret*-style wishful thinking has little therapeutic benefit. "I do not buy into the idea that one should always be optimistic—I view cognitive therapy as the power of realistic thinking. It's not simply wishing will make it so," he wrote in an e-mail in April 2007.

Accentuate the Positive

Martin Seligman, who is chairman of the Positive Psychology Center at the University of Pennsylvania, is well known in psychology circles for his experimental research on learned helplessness and optimism. He defines positive psychology as the "scientific study of the strengths and virtues that enable individuals and communities to thrive." It focuses on positive emotions, individual traits, and institutions. This new discipline is catching on. Often known as "Happiness 101," the courses are now taught at more than two hundred college campuses around the country. Seligman is careful to distinguish positive psychology from positive thinking. He likens the pursuit of positive feelings to hedonic theories of happiness, which talk about short-term emotional rushes that don't result in long-term happiness and meaning. Positive psychology looks at how individuals can use their strengths and talents to pursue challenging tasks that lead to the experience of flow (as described by Mihaly Csikszentmihalyi's bestselling 1990 book *Flow: The Psychology of Optimal Experience*), which in turn results in a fully engaged and meaningful life, that is, true happiness. Positive psychology is *not* about thinking everything is always going to be great, so full speed ahead. For example, Seligman says, you would not want an air traffic controller to feel overly optimistic about the prospects of your plane taking off in a storm. In the same way, a lone woman may be best served by feeling pessimistic about her chances of a pleasant evening when contemplating getting black-out drunk at a bar located in a dangerous part of town.

Positive psychology owes much to self-actualization, a psychological theory developed by Abraham Maslow in 1943. Maslow asserted that as soon as man meets his basic needs (food, shelter, safety), he seeks fulfillment of a pyramid of "higher" needs. At the top are needs that result in self-actualization: morality, creativity, and problem solving among them. Similarly, psychologist Carl Rogers—perhaps most famous for coining the expression "unconditional positive regard"—saw people as basically good (whereas Freud saw people as essentially neurotic). His fully functioning individual is open to experience, lives in the present, acknowledges freedom and takes responsibility for choices, and explores creativity (not necessarily artistic creativity, it could be as simple as doing the best job possible when confronted with a task).

All three theories suppose a healthy person has the ability to experience life fully and to achieve his or her "personal best." Fully actualized people can surely have so-called negative experiences but their outlook on life make them less prone to wallow in bad luck or defeat. It's perfectly reasonable, therefore, to say that people who subscribe to the law of attraction and truly believe their positive thoughts attract positive things are better positioned to become fully actualized than are nonbelievers or pessimists.

Punctuate the Negative

The idea that even one "negative" thought results in attraction of disappointment, loss, illness, disaster, or tragedy rightly troubles many people. According to Byrne, the law of attraction says that to be the victim of some horrendous event, such as a holocaust, a tsunami, a slaughter, or even just loss of a job, you have to be on the same frequency as that event, even if you were not specifically thinking about it. I'm not sure exactly what this means, but the idea seems to be that, in fact, you attracted whatever befell you.

Saying that disasters happen as a result of a population's negative thinking falls into religious fundamentalist territory: New Orleans was hit hard because of its population of sinners; the tsunami in Indonesia is a result of its people's savagery; 9/11 happened because the West is too liberal and God is displeased. We've heard fiery extremist religious leaders of every stripe say such things. This is deeply flawed logic, a slope none of us should want to slip down, but several people I talked to admitted privately that they believed there is some validity to the idea that the Jews attracted the Holocaust and blacks are responsible for the racism they experience.

As for why war, strife, and man's inhumanity to man occurs, there seems to be a consensus among a lot of believers I talked to that is best articulated by John Demartini. "There are seven areas that show up in every society and in every person: intellect, culture, vocation, finance, social, spiritual, and health. Any time a person or a society is disempowered in five of those areas, they will be overpowered. I guarantee if you look at any society that has been suppressed, you will see a lack of intellectual, vocational, financial, and physical strength. Look at Afghanistan—the Taliban were able to take over because there was a lack of intellectual, financial, and social power in the population. And they were physically isolated."

World problems aside, personal negativity does seem to have genuine value. Author and *Secret* contributor John Gray says that life has its ups and downs and there is little to be gained in pretending otherwise. "Learn to acknowledge the negative thought and move on. That is a discipline. Also remember that anyone who has created anything started with a positive thought—it takes hard work and effort, yes, but it starts with an optimistic perspective, and people take that for granted."

It has been pointed out to me more than once that while they may believe in the law of attraction, the speakers involved in *The Secret* do not sit around waiting for riches to fly through their windows. They are, to a person, motivated and hardworking. John Demartini is only half-joking when he says he is on the road speaking and working "four hundred days a year."

Ellen Langer points out that when people make a concerted effort to "think positive," they give credence to the negative thought.

"That which you call positive is something you are mindlessly drawn to; that which you say is negative is something you are mindlessly drawn away from," she says. Instead of labeling thoughts as one or the other, she recommends not judging a thought or an event in terms of good versus bad.

"If I asked you if you want to meet my friend Susan, and told you she was very impulsive, you may perceive 'impulsive' as negative and perhaps you would not want to meet her. If I told you Susan was spontaneous, that may be perceived as good and you would be excited to meet her. But they are really the same thing. Until you meet Susan you really have no idea whether she is worth knowing. The more mindful you are, the less judgmental you are—so it's not a matter of good or bad. It depends on how an idea or an event is understood.

"People pay lip service to the idea that everything is either positive or negative—but what they really mean is that everything has parts to it that are positive and negative. Byrne did a disservice by turning people off with the idea that no negative thoughts are allowed because they destroy your chances of getting what you want. If you want to experience what we consider to be positive, it's important not to be *evaluative,*" advises Langer. Of course, the caveat is that this theory is most useful in Western culture. It would be a very difficult argument to make in modern Darfur and tsunami-ravaged Indonesia.

John Demartini has a similar but less academic approach to the positive-negative issue than Langer does, but in many ways the inspirational speaker and the Harvard professor share a similar philosophy. "The reason people have negative thoughts is because of our addiction to fantasy and the feeling it gives us—fantasy of what love is, what life should be like," says Demartini. "We become manic when we see events or people as good or bad. I do not see this as productive. Our consciousness can never think something positive without having a negative comparison."

Demartini uses a neutralizing technique in his Breakthrough Experience workshop to show people that what they think is positive isn't, and what they think is negative isn't. The day I was scheduled to interview Demartini he also invited me to sit in on a workshop he was holding in New York City. It was my first self-improvement workshop (although I have gone on retreats at Dai Bosatsu Zendo—very different from what Demartini offers). Having experienced it, I can see why it is effective for many people.

The inspirational speaker may not put it this way, but Demartini's mission in life is to help people get over themselves. Instead of wallowing in the emotions and experiences that "push our buttons" and interfere with our ability to reach goals and enjoy life, he wants workshop participants to defuse emotional connections to past events and people so they can acknowledge them without having a meltdown. This is an admirable goal, since so many people in the modern world live through their self-perceived victim status, which lets them off the hook by blaming others for their failings. No self-reflection required—no need to take responsibility for your action: I cannot get a job because people are racist. I can't get promoted because my boss doesn't like me. I can't have a decent relationship because my mother mistreated me. I'm adopted so I can't relate to other people. I came from a broken home so I am allowed to be selfish. And so on. "We're all essentially the same," says Demartini, and half the battle is showing people that thinking their issues are "special" holds them back instead of propelling them forward. It interferes with their chance to experience flow.

Part of Demartini's process requires you to sit for hours writing down both sides of every person, event, and memory you can think of so you can see, at the end of an exhausting weekend, that what you thought was simply "good" or "bad" is no such thing. In the process you learn to be less evaluative, as Langer would say, of what happens to you in the future, and in doing so, you open yourself up to more experiences. It's true that when we prejudge a situation or person we close ourselves off from experience and perhaps opportunity. If that is what *The Secret* is supposed to be about, I'm all for it.

At the very least, the key to negativity seems to be in how you look at it. Arielle Ford relates the parable of the farmer who has a healthy son. His neighbor visits him and remarks on how lucky he is to have such a robust child. The farmer replies, "Maybe." Then the young man breaks his leg, and the neighbor consoles the father, saying, "Oh, it's terrible he had that accident." "Maybe," the farmer replies. Shortly afterward, the king calls every healthy young man into the army to fight a bloody war. The farmer's son can't enlist because of his broken leg. "If you talk to anyone who has gone through a crisis, if they are honest, they will tell you they are grateful they suffered," says Ford.

John Gray points out that if you walk through your life and deny the negative, you have no "juice" left with which to create. "People who are cruising along doing fine are not challenged. Part of what was missing from *The Secret* is that life does not always bring you what you hope to get. You have to prepare to be disappointed; that's part of the process of living." That disappointment can urge the healthy person on to greater deeds and accomplishments. Learning how to cope with and use disappointment may be the real secret to a successful life.

Darren E. Sherkat, a professor of sociology at Southern Illinois University at Carbondale, specializes in social movements and religion. He says there is another side of positive and negative outlooks that should be considered. There is a correlation between being happy and making cognitive errors or inaccurate thinking. "People who are happy are often mistaken. They can be given correct information and ignore it. It is called a 'fundamental attribution error,' or the tendency to overemphasize personality-based explanations for behaviors observed in others while underemphasizing the role and power of circumstances on the same behavior. You can find similar cognitive errors among highly religious people," Sherkat says. "They tend to systematically ignore information or misremember facts in a systematic way. Acting like things are positive when things suck is a really silly idea, and not helpful in the real world. It actually does not give people a sense of calm with their own circumstances."

Practice Makes Perfection: Laura Smith

Enough about theory—there are people who live the law of attraction and swear by it. Some may call them high-achieving optimists. Laura Smith, the director of programming for the health and wellness multimedia company Lime Radio in New York, is one such person.

"*The Secret* is today's version of a line of thinking that's very old," says Smith, who started her New Thought quest after college. "I found a Christian Science pamphlet in Grand Central Station that explained there was an operating force in everyone's life that is all good, and that we all have the power to create miracles." That discovery was the beginning of Smith's interest in metaphysics, which led her to the work of Louise Hay and Esther and Jerry Hicks. Smith eventually found her way to the Love Center in California, described as a nonprofit educational organization that raises love awareness. Founders Scott and Shannon Peck asked

Smith to write down a highly detailed description of her idea of the perfect day, including what she would do, where she would go, and whom she would talk to. "It forced me to be very clear about what I wanted. That was five years ago, and when I look at what I described it is where I am right now," says Smith. "I am in a tall building in New York City creating media that heals the world—and five years ago there was no such media as that."

Smith has done voice-over work for twenty years and started doing radio work at a community station in Greenwich, Connecticut. "Everything I learned at that station put me where I am today in terms of my career. I did not know that when I wrote down my perfect day it was a literal and actual trigger that put me where I am now." While working in Greenwich, Smith stumbled across a company called Wisdom Radio in Bluefield, West Virginia. She took a job with the company, and it was subsequently bought by investors who changed the name to Lime as a way of reaching out to a more mainstream audience. Satellite powerhouse Sirius now broadcasts it from Manhattan.

Smith says her perfect-day account was so specific and so accurate that at one point she walked into the office of her boss at Lime Radio and realized that it was the exact room she had described in her scenario.

The programmer says written affirmations also helped her achieve her goal. "I read in a book that writing about what you want in the present tense and then reading it many times during the day helps manifestation." At the time her goal was to move from Connecticut to New York as a music jock. "So I wrote out 'I am at LITE FM and LOVING IT,' and she did, in fact, get a jock job at LITE FM, where she can still be heard on weekends. "I have to imagine there were hundreds of applicants for that job," she says—so what made her stand apart from the rest? Soon after, she wrote affirmations about working at Sirius, and that desire also came to fruition. "I am always very specific and write down what is my heart. It is a declaration to the universe, seen by the unseen world. I believe in that and think it helps bring my dreams about."

The affirmations may have helped her send out the confidence vibes to her interviewer, which Dr. Howard Brody talked about earlier. To be sure, Smith's drive, enthusiasm, and energy are evident when you hear her talk—no small feat when navigating the often-tumultuous waters of show biz *and* single motherhood. Her attitude clearly gives her a leg up on the competition, and it's hard to argue that her beliefs, affirmations, and thoughts have not played a part in her success and happiness.

As someone deeply familiar with the nuances of the law of attraction, she sees the greatest downfall of *The Secret* as its lack of two important ideas. The first is the necessity to release your dream once you have asked for it. "It's ask, believe, receive, and *let go!* That's what most other books say and this is left out of Rhonda's book." Some psychologists call the not letting go "excessive rumination"—thinking about and replaying an idea over and over again to the point that it actually hinders your ability to act on it.

Second, Smith offers the important reminder for people to practice the law of attraction for the greater good of everyone. "The law exists for your advantage, but it comes across [in *The Secret*] that the effect on other people doesn't matter. There is nothing wrong with manifesting a bicycle, but it is not simply about getting what you want. You can tell your kid to manifest a bike, but it cannot happen by taking it away from someone else; so there needs to be some mention that getting what you want should not be detrimental. On the other hand I am grateful for those people who find *The Secret* comforting if they have lost the concept that life is good. So many people have the mind-set that being happy is for other people, and it's not."

So . . . Does It Work?

Yes, for the people who say it works. Just like Christianity "works" for Christians, Judaism "works" for Jews, yoga for yogis, and Wicca for witches. For the rest of us, curmudgeons included, there are no absolutes—our behavior, if not our thoughts and perceptions, attract and repel things, people, and events. Being more observant of what's going on in our lives is not such a bad idea. At any rate, the brain is capable of so much more than is outlined here (and you can scratch the surface with me in Chapter 5). But there *are* a few secrets that make life better but won't turn you into a court jester:

1. Accept your flaws and don't dwell on them.
2. Adopt an optimistic outlook, which is different from positive thinking.
3. Be a realist—don't live through your fantasies.
4. Show some gratitude for what you have.
5. Don't prejudge people or situations.
6. Observe what's going on around you.
7. Manifest reasonable dreams by acting on them.
8. Relax.
9. Maintain social ties.
10. Care—for yourself and others.
11. Laugh.

Part II

❧

The Ideas
Behind
the Secret

This look at the philosophical, scientific, and theological ideas behind the law of attraction is far from exhaustive. In this section we look at the fine threads of ideas, physics, and world religions that form a multifarious blanket of inspiration and imitation of old self-help literature, misinterpretations and contextualization of complex scientific and mathematical concepts, and the refashioning of religious ideas from hard-to-swallow dogma into sweet-tasting secular candy.

The idea for *The Secret* started when Rhonda Byrne read Wallace D. Wattles's 1910 *The Science of Getting Rich*. Since little is known about Wattles, we can only examine the words he actually wrote and what was going on in the United States when he wrote them, in the early twentieth century.

Wattles was a man of his time. He wrote about New Thought, a popular subject with other writers of the time as well. New Thought blended philosophy with then-current strides in science to advance the idea that health, wealth, and happiness could be attained through the control of conscious and nonconscious beliefs, attitudes, and expectations—that is, the law of attraction. These ideas caught on again during the Depression, washing in and over a whole new set of writers and readers—which include, most prominently, Napoleon Hill and his classic *Think and Grow Rich,* one of the best-selling books of all time—and again in the 1960s, the 1980s, and of course now. But New Thought started in the nineteenth century, and hasn't changed much from that time.

Science—specifically physics, cellular biology, and neuroscience—is frequently summoned as proof that the law of attraction is a universal law or a physical law. Yet even the physicists who participated in *The Secret* have clarified the interpretation of their stances on these matters. And some physicists don't see any connection at all between physics and the ability to find a parking spot in Manhattan whenever one is needed. *The Secret* also says that Christianity, Buddhism, and Judaism bolster its claims. While Byrne limits references to the Bible or to Christ, perhaps for fear of turning secular people off, the law of attraction is very much biblical in nature. There are also tenuous connections to contemporary Western interpretations of Buddhist philosophy and Jewish mysticism and kabbalah.

Wallace Wattles & Co.

The Science of Getting Rich by Wallace D. Wattles ignited an idea in Rhonda Byrnes, the outcome of which would have doubtless pleased Wattles had he been around to see the success of *The Secret*. His books remain in print, and are freely available on the Internet at www.ferguson-assoc.com, giving the lie to the claim that the law of attraction had been previously hoarded and hidden.

To be sure, Wattles's ideas represented a whole movement of thought focused on the science and power of the mind, which was widely dispersed not only in the United States but also all over Europe during the late nineteenth and early twentieth centuries. Its appeal has waxed and waned over the intervening years, but its central theme, the law of attraction, has been a mainstay of the New Age and metaphysical movement for many years. Wattles's idea, which was not original, owes a small and indirect debt to Benjamin Franklin and William James, whom I talked about in Chapter 2. The law of attraction specifically is also rooted in newer ideas that rose during the uncertain and rapidly changing times that characterized both the industrial revolution and World War I.

Wattles: International Man of Mystery

The law of attraction may not have been a secret, but what does seem to be hidden is detailed biographical information about Wallace Wattles. Despite the popularity of his books, the man himself is obscure. The only photo of him, widely available on the Internet, is of a narrow-faced man with an outsized proboscis. According to a letter his daughter Florence wrote to one of his publishers after his death, Wattles was born a Methodist in 1860, was somewhat frail, especially later in life, and died in 1911, just one year after the publication of *The Science of Getting Rich*. He hailed from the Midwest, eventually settling in Indiana.

The name "Wattles" is itself uncommon, but not unique. Whitepages.com has 293 listings for people named Wattles today, and they are scattered across the United States. Any one of them could be a distant relative of Wally, as his fans refer to him. And given the recent interest in Wattles's books, it would come as no surprise if they started coming out of the woodwork to stake a claim.

There are no contemporaneous newspaper accounts of Wallace to be found on LexisNexis, or ProQuest, the historical archives of *The New York Times*. This suggests that Wattles was not especially prominent in the science of the mind movement, since the *Times* did cover the lecture circuit, and went out of its way to list participants and speakers. There are no entries in new or old versions of the *Encyclopedia Britannica*, or the *Columbia Encyclopedia*. The Mormons, famous for their massive collection of genealogical information, have no record of either Wallace Wattles or his daughter Florence. The Mormons pursue general genealogy for theological reasons. They believe that helping Mormons and non-Mormons alike preserve family records is a religious mandate. This massive effort has resulted in the church's Family History Library, with a collection of about eight billion names. The Salt Lake City Library is the largest collection of genealogical records in the world. That's why it's odd that the Mormons would miss two Americans born over a hundred years ago, especially since one of them wrote books that continue to sell to this day and the other was active in Socialist Party politics. I could not come up with birth records; no official records of his existence could be found at all. However, the name Florence Wattles appears on lists of delegates to the Socialist Party National Committee in 1912 and 1915; it seems very likely this is Wattles's daughter, as will become evident later on.

Wattles: Limousine Liberal?

In the introduction to *The Science of Getting Rich,* Wattles says that Descartes, Spinoza, Leibniz, Schopenhauer, Hegel, and Emerson influenced his ideas. He may well have read their teachings, but it turns out that an introduction to Christian socialism first prompted him to start writing. Christian socialism is a blend of Christianity and left-wing politics, fusing their mutual interest in pursuit of an egalitarian and antiestablishment social order. It is anticapitalist—which is ironic, since Wattles's most popular book was about accumulating wealth. Funnier still, after years of near ruin, according to Florence, Wattles made lots of money during the last three years of his life speaking, writing, and selling books.

"For years his life was cursed by poverty and the fear of poverty," wrote Florence. "He was always scheming and planning to get for his family those things which make the abundant life possible." Poor as a post and desperate for a little inspiration to change his luck, one December day in 1896 Wattles traveled to a convention of reformers in Chicago to hear the popular speaker, George D. Herron. There, "he caught Herron's social vision," Florence continued. "From that day until his death he worked unceasingly to realize the glorious vision of human brotherhood."

Herron, a minister and a member of the Socialist Party, wrote numerous books and pamphlets on social and religious issues, including *The Christian State: A Political Vision of Christ* (1895; a 2001 reprint is available on Amazon), *The Menace of Peace* (1917), and *The Defeat in the Victory* (1921). Herron also financed the early writings of one-time Socialist Party member Upton Sinclair (who abandoned the party in 1934).

Herron started his career as a pastor in the Congregational Church in Lake City, Minnesota, and then moved to Iowa to preside over the First Congregational Church in Burlington. In 1893, Mrs. Carrie Rand, one of the founders of the Rand School and an active socialist, became friends with Herron, eventually marrying him after he divorced his first wife, and endowed for him a chair of Applied Christianity at Iowa College. Herron was a faculty member there until he resigned in 1900 under pressure— the university administration had had enough of his socialist activities. Shortly after his departure Herron renounced Christian socialism and became a member of the Socialist Party.

According to Robert M. Crunden's *Ministers of Reform: The Progressives' Achievement in American Civilization, 1889–1920*, Herron "was probably the most famous reform clergyman of his day and certainly the most publicized voice for reform within the church." At the turn of the nineteenth century, Crunden writes, religion provided the "central motivating force for adventurous thinking" related to secular matters. When the poverty-stricken Wattles heard Herron speak, he might have heard him suggest ideas inspired by Hegel and presented in *The Christian State:*

> The spiritual alone is the real and eternal.
>
> The consciousness of one's own mind and powers is being transcended by the race consciousness of one universal mind and spirit sovereign within all men, making them members of one another, and humanity a body of God.
>
> I need but to appeal to your intelligent consideration of history, to your consciousness of the world within you, and your observation of the world without, to have you confess with me that the world is far less institutionally governed than we commonly assume.
>
> Any scientific interpretation of history, any faithful analysis of progress, can end only in witnessing to the supreme fact of the unseen government of the world.

At any rate, Florence said her father was hooked: "The supreme faith of man never left him; never for a moment did he lose confidence in the power of the master Intelligence to right every wrong and to give every man and women his or her fair share of the good things in life."

From Socialism to New Thought

After Wattles absorbed Christian socialism, he moved to Elwood, Indiana, where he embraced to the New Thought movement and began writing regularly for one of its major journals of the day, *Nautilus.*

New Thought was contemporaneous with and loosely related to Christian socialism. It emphasized the attainment of health, wealth, and happiness through the control of conscious and unconscious beliefs, attitudes, and expectations—that is, the law of attraction. As one early leader, Sarah J. Farmer, wrote of the movement: "It is simply putting ourselves in new relation to the world about us by changing our thought concerning it. We are not creatures of circumstance; we are creators." Seductive words for common folk who wanted in on the great wealth that people like Jim Fisk, Jay Gould, and Cornelius Vanderbilt seemed to manifest without effort.

In *Each Mind a Kingdom: Women, Sexual Purity, and the New Thought Movement, 1875–1920,* author Beryl Satter, who does not mention Wattles in the book, writes that, according to the New Thought reformers' vision, "government could exist only if the people who made up its citizenry were virtuous, self-sacrificing, and economically independent (and so incorruptible)." Satter also sees New Thought as a way for its primarily white and middle-class (and female) adherents to achieve race perfection. "They believed that morally and physically perfect people would help save the republic from moral, political, and economic ruin." This makes sense given the fact that between 1866 and 1912, the United States absorbed more than twenty-five million people, mainly from Europe, in one of the largest waves of immigration the country has seen. Then, like now, foreign migration was a hot-button issue that left many in the middle class feeling uneasy.

The New Thought movement itself was no secret, and indeed the aggressive and enthusiastic marketing of its ideas via magazine articles, newspaper coverage, pamphlets, books, public demonstrations, and speeches echo the same marketing techniques employed by inspirational speakers today. New Thought writers wanted to spread the word to both gain converts and make money. The *last* thing they wanted to do was keep their ideas under wraps. Florence Wattles says that her father's Sunday-night lectures in Indianapolis were the family's only source of income for some time. It wouldn't have paid to keep his fantastic knowledge to himself.

New Thoughts from Old Ideas

Many of the central ideas of the New Thought movement are commonly attributed to New Hampshire native and Maine resident Phineas Parkhurst Quimby, born in 1802 to a blacksmith and his wife. Quimby believed that the mind and body interact with each other, an idea that at the time was considered radical and crazy, but today is accepted as a given. He also maintained that beliefs were as responsible for physical disease as biology, if not more so.

> Every disease is the invention of man, and has no identity in wisdom; but to those who believe it, it is a truth. If everything man does not understand were blotted out, what is there left, of man? Would he be better, or worse, if nine tenths of all he thinks he knows were blotted out of his mind, and he existed with what is true?

Four people helped spread Quimby's ideas and gave them the name New Thought: Warren Felt Evans, Annetta Seabury Dresser, Julius Dresser, and founder of the Christian Science movement Mary Baker Eddy (more on Baker Eddy in Chapter 6). Julius and Annetta Dresser and Mary Baker Eddy (nee Mary

Patterson) all received "mental healing" treatment from Quimby, which is how they all met. (Quimby and cohorts were influenced by the eighteenth-century scientist and philosopher Emanuel Swedenborg.)

Other self-helpers were working almost simultaneously with the New Thought group. Another hardy New Englander, Orison Swett Marden, wrote numerous self-help books, including *Pushing to the Front* (1894) and *How to Get What You Want* (1917). In 1897 he founded the New Thought magazine *Success;* it went out of business in 1912, but he started it up again in 1918. The first incarnation of the magazine had a circulation of half a million, large by the day's standards. Marden was influenced by Samuel Smiles, a Scotsman, who had written a book called *Self-Help* in 1859 that encouraged the idea of individual achievement. He followed it with books extolling various virtues: *Character, Thrift, Duty,* and *Life and Labour*.

The first incarnation of *Success* magazine included a mix of New Thought, science, religion, moneymaking tips, etiquette, fashion and grooming advice, and guidance for modern women who couldn't decide whether it was worth working if they didn't actually need the cash. For example, the February 1904 issue included these entries: "How Wall Street Makes Something out of Nothing" (subtitle: "The Manner in Which Some Notable Combines Have Burst Because of Too Much Water and Indigestible Securities, and How a Foolish Public Is the Loser Thereby"), by David Graham Phillips; "Superiority, the Best Trade Mark," by Orison Swett Marden; and "A Plea for Good Manners," by Mrs. Burton Kingsland. In the July 1903 issue, you can read "The Requiem of the Has Beens," by Owne Kildare; "The Habit of Not Feeling Well," by Orison Swett Marden; and "Suggestions in Dress," by Marion Bell.

Nautilus was another leading New Thought journal, published from the turn of the century through the early 1950s by Mrs. Elizabeth Struble (later, Towne). According to her obituary in *The New York Times* (June 2, 1960), at the height of its popularity the magazine had a circulation of ninety thousand.

Originally from Oregon, Elizabeth Struble found herself a single mother after a youthful marriage crumbled. She was the personification of pluck. In 1898, with an investment of $30, she founded a New Thought pamphlet called *Nautilus* as a way to make extra money for her family. In 1900, she moved it and her two children from Oregon to Holyoke, Massachusetts. There, she met, married, and took the name of a successful book and magazine publisher and distributor, William E. Towne. With his financial help she was able to create a profitable New Thought publishing company.

Towne enticed many of the best-known New Thought writers to write for *Nautilus.* She ran pieces by Wallace Wattles in almost every issue during the early 1900s. The bylines of Ella Wheeler Wilcox, Horatio W. Dresser (son of Annetta and Julius), and Orison Swett Marden can also be found in early copies. She also distributed books by New Thought authors—like a modern-day Hay House or Beyond Words (the publisher of *The Secret,* which is now owned by Simon & Schuster).

She also wrote several books. Her 1902 autobiography, *Experiences in Self-Healing,* which covered just twenty years of her amazing life, sold one hundred thousand copies—very good even by today's standards. Her 1903 *Joy Philosophy* contains the following passage, showing clear links to the law of attraction:

> This alternation from Being to Doing—from I AM to I DO—is the secret of power and progress and success. It is

the soul's breathing. You inhale in the world I AM; you ex-
hale in the world I DO. The more easily and regularly you
vibrate between these two the more complete is your real-
ization of health and success.

When you have that tired and unsuccessful feeling due
to too much exhaling in the world I DO, just rise into the
realm I AM and by imagination and affirmation pump
yourself full of—I AM power. I AM wisdom. I AM love. I
AM what I desire to be. ALL Things work together for the
manifestation of what I AM.

Towne was a feminist and celebrity of her own making. Not
only did she support herself for several years with her New
Thought pamphlets, she was the driving force behind the company that bore her name, Elizabeth Towne Company, established
well before the Nineteenth Amendment was ratified in 1920. She
was a tireless speaker and turned up at many New Thought as-
semblies. On July 2, 1905, the *Times* reported that Towne would
speak about "The Wellspring of Success Within Us" at the annual
meeting of the National Business Women's League at the Endi-
cott Hotel in Manhattan. She was the president of the International New Thought Alliance in 1924, assumed editorship of its
Bulletin, and during her tenure managed to double its size from a
sixteen-page pamphlet to a thirty-two-page magazine.

In 1928, the *New York Times* reported on Towne's mayoral
bid in Holyoke. If elected, she promised to "put civic service in
the saddle instead of profits for the gang, which has ridden
roughshod through every administration under every mayor for
as far back as I have political remembrances." She stated confi-
dently that "the only hope for a change to open politics for all of
us is to try as Mayor the one independent, practical, and politics-
wise woman of Holyoke who offers herself, namely, Elizabeth

Towne." She lost. Towne operated *Nautilus* until 1951 and died in a Holyoke nursing home on June 1, 1960, at age ninety-five.

Secret Members of the New Thought Gang

In *The Secret* Byrne includes profiles of, and quotes from, other popular New Thought writers: Charles Haanel (1866–1949); Genevieve Behrend (c. 1881–1960); Robert Collier (1885–1950); and the earlier Prentice Mulford (1834–1891). Like metaphysical writers and speakers of today, they crisscrossed each other with similar ideas and tried their best to promote their beliefs to as many people as they could through the sale of pamphlets and by giving lectures. Speeches that were open to the public at no cost were often a venue for selling pamphlets at the back of the room, all of which helped brand their personalities, a strategy still in use today. The brief excerpts of their work I quote here demonstrate similar lines of thinking that existed among them, and also with today's metaphysical writers. Indeed, many writers have simply coopted this earlier work and put their name on it. Some of the books, including Wattles's, may have fallen into obscurity over the years not because of a conspiracy to keep their information from public view but because of cyclical disinterest. And frankly, none of them, with perhaps the exception of Mulford, were ever considered to be important writers or thinkers in their own day. They were considered part of a trend that proved to be fleeting, like so many trends are. Luckily, reprints of many of their books are still available today and can be ordered online, and some are free on the Internet.

When Byrne says in *The Secret* that law of attraction information was expensive, she may have been referring to businessman Charles Haanel's *The Master Key System*, which he developed in

1912 as a twenty-four-week course, for which he charged $1,500. This was a great deal of money at the time, but today it is available for free on the Internet at www.psitek.net/pages/PsiTek TMKSContents.html; it is also available in book form from Amazon for about $15. In 1922, he wrote *Mental Chemistry,* which included chapters on "suggesting" illness and pain from your life, and how your mind can influence luck and destiny.

Haanel was a successful businessman, born in Ann Arbor, Michigan, on May 22, 1866. At one point he made his way to Mexico and convinced investors to buy land in Tehuantepec for sugar and coffee plantations. The company was formed in 1898, and he was named president. In 1905, Haanel merged the firm with six other companies and formed the Continental Commercial Company. He also helped form the Sacramento Valley Improvement Company, owned and controlled a large Tokay vineyard, and presided over the Mexico Gold & Silver Mining Company. Unlike the Christian socialist William Wattles, Haanel was a Republican. Yet both were drawn to New Thought and both used it as a philosophy of moneymaking. It bridged all gaps, even political ones. Haanel wrote several New Thought pamphlets and books, including *The New Psychology* and *The Amazing Secrets of the Yogi. Master Key* is by far his most famous, and marketing the information in a week-by-week subscription course was clearly a stroke of business genius.

In lesson 4 of *The Master Key System* he writes:

> Thought is energy and energy is power, and it is because all the religions, sciences and philosophies with which the world has heretofore been familiar have been based upon the manifestation of this energy instead of the energy itself, that the world has been limited to effects, while causes have been ignored or misunderstood. For this reason we have

God and the Devil in religion, positive and negative in science, and good and bad in philosophy.

Genevieve Behrend, another popular New Thought writer quoted as an expert in *The Secret,* studied with Thomas Troward (1847–1916), a follower of mental science who originally hailed from India, where his English father was a colonel in the Indian army. He wrote for an English New Thought publication called *Expressions* and gave lectures on mental science throughout the United Kingdom. Harvard professor and psychologist William James was familiar with Troward's work and noted that his Edinburgh lectures on mental science were "far and away the ablest statement of philosophy I have met, beautiful in its sustained clearness of thought and style, a really classic statement."

Behrend studied with Troward for a couple of years. Then, around 1915, she opened a New Thought school in New York City called the School of the Builders and ran it until 1925. After that she established a similar school in Los Angeles, and then for the next thirty-five years she hit the road as a full-time itinerant lecturer on mental science and New Thought. *Your Invisible Power,* written in 1921 and still in print, was her first book. Less than one hundred pages long, its chapter titles include, "How to Attract to Yourself the Things You Desire" and "How I Attracted to Myself Twenty Thousand Dollars." In it she writes:

> The power within you which enables you to form a thought picture is the starting point of all there is. In its original state it is the undifferentiated formless substance of life. Your thought picture forms the mold (so to speak) into which this formless substance takes shape. . . . The joyous assurance with which you make your picture is the very powerful magnet of Faith, and nothing can obliterate it. You are happier

than you ever were, because you have learned to know where your course of supply is, and you rely upon its never-failing response to your given direction.

Joe Vitale, one of the modern-day experts featured in *The Secret,* republished one of Behrend's books, *Attaining Your Desires by Letting Your Subconscious Mind Work for You,* under the slightly altered title *How to Attain Your Desires by Letting Your Subconscious Mind Work for You, Vol. 1.* The headline on the back cover of the book reads: "Fiery Texas author breathes life into dead woman." Underneath, Vitale is described as a "world-famous copywriter" who created the "hypnotic writing" method—which is a technique having to do with composing effective sales and marketing copy and letters.

In the introduction to the original book, Behrend writes:

> Thought-power is the kingdom of God in us, always creating results in our physical forms corresponding to our normal sustained thought. As Troward has said, "Thought is the only action of the mind. By your habitual thoughts you create corresponding external physical conditions, because you thereby create the nucleus which attracts to itself its own correspondence, in due order, until the finished work is manifested on the material plane." This is the principle upon which we shall proceed to work out a simple and rational basis of thought and action whereby we may bring into outer expression any desired goal.

The third well-known New Thought writer mentioned in *The Secret* is Robert Collier. Collier was born on April 19, 1885, in St. Louis with a silver pen in his mouth. His father, John Collier, traveled frequently and for long periods of time as a foreign correspondent for *Collier's Magazine,* which was founded and published by his brother, Robert's uncle, Peter F. Collier. Robert went to seminary with the intention of entering the clergy, but decided against it and instead headed to West Virginia to make his own way before eventually joining the family business. He found work as a mining engineer and studied business correspondence and advertising in his spare time. Like Joe Vitale, he eventually became a copywriter. Eight years after moving to West Virginia, Collier went east to New York and joined his uncle's firm, in the advertising department of the P. F. Collier Publishing Company.

Robert, like Wallace Wattles, was sickly. Since his illness could not be pinpointed, or treated via conventional methods, he sought help and an eventual cure from Christian Science. This got him interested in both health food and New Thought. Like Rhonda Byrne, he delved into New Thought literature and philosophy, and saw not only personal fulfillment but a business opportunity. Collier synthesized these "practical psychology" ideas and, in 1926, compiled them into a set of books called *The Secret of the Ages* (still in print as one volume). Within six months he had sold over three hundred thousand sets. Seeing the market, he wrote four more books, or "courses" in New Thought: *The God in You, The Secret Power, The Magic Word,* and *The Law of the Higher Potential.*

Collier died in 1950. A year before, in 1949, he published *Be Rich! The Science of Getting What You Want,* in which he wrote the following. It is reminiscent of a scene from *The Secret* that shows Aladdin rubbing an oil lamp to conjure his desire-granting genie.

Here is the secret of riches and success that has been buried 1,900 years deep. Since time began, mankind has been searching for this secret. It has been found—*and lost again*—a score of times. The Ancients of all the races have had some inkling of it, as is proven by the folktales and legends that have come down to us, like the story of Aladdin and his wonderful lamp, or Ali Baba and his "Open Sesame" to the treasure trove.

Of all of the New Thinkers included in *The Secret,* Prentice Mulford is perhaps the most compelling. A contemporary of Mark Twain, he was born in Sag Harbor, New York, sometime between 1835 and 1840, according to a June 1, 1891, obituary and account of his life in *The New York Times.* Before Mulford got interested in and started writing about New Thought he had already lived a colorful and very full, if not rough-and-tumble, life. It's worth hearing about, not only because it contrasts with what little is known of Wattles, who seemed to be desperate in his own way to find something that would both add meaning to his life and money to his wallet, but also shows Mulford as a seeker—someone perfectly positioned to be drawn in by "mind science."

As a young boy Mulford hung around the ships and sailors that frequented the whaling harbor near his home, doubtless soaking up the seamen's tales of adventure and travel. Eventually he caught gold fever and made his way to San Francisco in 1855 during the Gold Rush on the clipper ship *Wizard.* Once in the city by the bay, he worked as a cook and steward on the schooner *Henry,* which was bound for Southern California. Once there, the young teenager spent a few unsuccessful years trying to mine gold. After that he taught in a mining camp in Tuolumne County, California.

When the copper-mining craze started in 1862, Mulford staked a claim near a town appropriately named Copperopolis. During the ten years that mining was active in the town he made and lost a very small fortune. Undeterred, when he heard about a silver discovery in Nevada, he pulled up stakes and traveled there, where he formed the Mulford Mining, Prospecting, and Land Company. The company went under in less than one year, and Mulford was back to square one, penniless but still determined to make something of himself. He *walked* back to southern California, almost freezing to death in the process.

After several tough weeks of travel, and safely back in Sonora, he got a job as a post-hole digger. To amuse his fellow workers, he composed a comedic speech, likely about the work they did, which apparently pleased his colleagues. Their enthusiasm made Mulford realize he had a natural gift for gab, so he turned his talents to writing and became an itinerant comedian. In 1865, he heard about New Thought and developed an interest in its theories. One year later, he considered and then abandoned the idea of running for local political office; instead he began writing letters to the editor of a weekly San Francisco paper called *Golden Era,* often under the name "Dogberry." The editor was so impressed with his missives that he offered him a job, eventually making him editor in chief of the paper.

Mulford freelanced for several other newspapers and magazines, and around 1882, he moved to New York, where he became the editor of the New York *Graphic.* He continued to freelance for San Francisco papers, covering the 1876 Philadelphia Centennial Exposition, and the Paris and Vienna Expositions. He lived for a time in London, reporting from there. He also wrote his autobiography, *Life by Land and Sea,* and another book called *The Swamp Angel.*

Because he had by this time become well known as a journalist and adventurer, and his interest in New Thought had become a serious pursuit, he began to write science of the mind essays, some thirty-seven of which were published in *White Cross Magazine,* another New Thought publication; many of these have been collected in a book that is still available today. His topics included "Laws of Marriage," "The Slavery of Fear," and "The Art of Forgetting." He also gave lectures on New Thought as well as culture and history. For instance, in 1875 he gave a lecture at New York's Liberal Club on "The Underlying Causes of Intemperance." In 1876, he gave a lecture on the Chinese in California at Trinity Chapel in New York.

According to another *Times* account of Mulford's life (December 9, 1891), it was in London that the newspaperman met a young girl who would change his life. Essentially a street urchin, the sixteen-year-old approached him to buy a newspaper. After talking to the girl, he discovered she was an orphan "living in a garret." He took an interest in her and arranged for a wealthy female friend to support and educate her. According to Jim Gillis, a former miner in Sonora and friend of Mulford, the girl "became a brilliant scholar, and grew very beautiful." When she was nineteen, Mulford married her and took her back to New York, where, according to the story, she fooled around with another man and Mulford found out. Heartbroken, he gave her all his savings, $5,000, and they went their separate ways. The young woman took only half the money and never saw him again, although they were never legally divorced.

Depressed, Mulford went back to California for a while, where Jim Gillis says he preferred getting drunk to writing, although he did hammer out a few "syndicate letters." A lecture of indeterminate topic was arranged in 1890, which he gave, but then returned east for the last time.

His body was found in a canoe floating in Sheepshead Bay,

Brooklyn, in May of 1891. It went unidentified for several days. F. J. Needham, the man who published Mulford's New Thought essays, identified the writer. The boat was described as "being within easy reach of assistance and where the sound of his voice could have been heard ashore." A week earlier he had parted from Needham with the promise of a job to write a regular weekly column for his *White Cross Magazine.*

Needham said that Mulford was well and happy, but "needed solitude in which to finish his work, so he determined to combine business and pleasure by making a trip in his canoe from this city to his old house in Sag Harbor." The publisher said this was not unusual for Mulford, who, when he wasn't living with the publisher, stayed in his canoe, "eating and sleeping there." He was found with $25 in his pocket, and his boat was well-stocked with food, clothing, an oil stove, a bottle of St. Croix rum, and blankets, along with artist's materials and writing implements. "Mulford liked this nomadic sort of life, and as he had nobody to care for, he paddled, sailed, and drifted aimlessly about as best suited him." His body was clean and unmarked—no poison was found on board the boat, but that did not mean there wasn't any in his system. At the time, the theory was that he had died either of an undiagnosed heart disease or apoplexy . . . or possibly suicide.

Indeed, after his death, Mulford's friends described his "weak point" as his interest in "spiritualism and kindred fancies," which he was exposed to as a reporter. A rambling group of letters found in the canoe refer to the "spirit" that was watching over him, promising brighter days ahead. After Mulford's death, Needham published the *White Cross* essays in a series of several pamphlets with titles such as "Thoughts Are Things," "Force and How to Get It," "The God in Yourself," and "How to Push Your

Business." In what turned out to be an act of prescience, Mulford wrote the following in "Thoughts Are Things," in 1889, just a few years before his death:

> The science of happiness lies in controlling our thought and getting thought from sources of healthy life. When your mind is diverted from possibly the long habit of thinking and living in the gloomy side of things and admitting gloomy thoughts, you will find to your surprise that the very place the sight of which gave you pain will give you pleasure. Because you have banished a certain unhealthy mental condition into which you before allowed yourself to drift.

Byrne is right that the secret is old information; it's stunning how closely the ideas of metaphysical writers working today mirror the New Thought writers. Striking too is the way in which each generation's "teachers" made their living similarly— as itinerant speakers, self-publishers, and workshop leaders. A good marketing model never dies.

· 5 ·

What the @%&*$ Does Science
Have to Do with the Secret?

There is something fascinating about science. One
gets such wholesale returns of conjecture out of such
a trifling investment of fact.

— MARK TWAIN

BELIEVERS IN THE law of attraction regularly cite physics, molecular biology, neurology, and other complex disciplines as literal proof that our thoughts alone can produce specific outcomes.
The Secret says that quantum physics "tells us that the entire Universe emerged from thought!" and therefore our thoughts hold
cosmic power. Not true, according to quantum physicists, including those who were featured in both *The Secret* and the related
film *What the Bleep.*

For example, physicist Fred Alan Wolf, who is featured in
both films, says that much of what he said when interviewed for
The Secret was left on the cutting-room floor. "The scientific basis that was mentioned was botched and all that got out was a
simplified idea, a little more than an infomercial. I was dismayed
because I had lots of interesting things to say, but I did not say the
law of attraction is based on physics. There is absolutely nothing

in physics that says just because you desire something you will attract it into your life."

In fact, Wolf writes the complete opposite in the new and updated section of his book *Taking the Quantum Leap:* "Quantum mechanics *seems to point to the limits of human power.* These limits refer to our knowledge and our ability to gain knowledge." A little while later he writes, "Certainly, if people became aware that a power over another human being was impossible because of quantum physics, the world would be a different place." And further on he writes, "Thus we become helpless, feel inadequate, *and long for the order we are helpless to create in the universe.* All we can do is go along with it." (Italics are mine.)

David Z. Albert, who is director of Columbia University's Philosophical Foundations of Physics and author of *Quantum Mechanics and Experience* and *Time and Chance,* both featured in *What the Bleep,* has said in published newspaper reports that his words were edited to make it sound as if he believed in the law of attraction. He does not. In the September 16, 2004, issue of *Salon* (dir.salon.com/story/ent/feature/2004/09/16/bleep/index_np.html) Albert stated definitively that positive thinking does not alter the structure of the world around us.

> I am, indeed, profoundly unsympathetic to attempts at linking quantum mechanics with consciousness. Moreover, I explained all that, at great length, on camera, to the producers of the film. . . . Had I known that I would have been so radically misrepresented in the movie, I would certainly not have agreed to be filmed.

Yet, apart from physics, in the sense that we use our minds to invent, dream, and then act, we do create our reality. But this is very different from the idea that we impact the order of the universe or move objects with our thoughts. For instance, if we indulge our temptation to punch the human resources manager during an interview, we "create the reality" of not getting the job, and maybe even of going to jail for assault. Even if we do not follow through on our desire, if our anger is evident to the HR gal, we might not get the job. But if we conceal our feelings from her, there's a good chance that, if we are qualified, the job is ours.

Let's say a composer takes a trip between New York and Boston on Amtrak. The clacking of the train on the tracks inspires a tune, and he jots down a few phrases or notes on the back of an envelope. Back home, he plays the tune on his piano, making further notations on music paper. He gives the song to his fellow musicians, and they record the tune and perform it at a concert. The composer's original thought has indeed created music that is tangible on paper, on a CD, and as sound in the air. People who hear the music have new thoughts, and perhaps they are inspired to create something in their own lives. This is called the end result of acting on our imagination.

But this is not what Byrne and other believers are talking about. They are saying that when you think about something, the thought is sent into the universe and alters the state of the world, with no other steps required on your part. That means that the notes in the composer's head might be heard in fully formed unity on the radio the day after he thought of them. This might happen, of course, if the clacking of the train on the tracks *reminded* the composer of a song *already recorded*. When he hears it the next day, *The Secret* follower would say, ah-ha, the composer "created" the playing of the song by the disc jockey. Not a coincidence. Not probability. The law of attraction.

Actually, psychology has a name for believers' view that coincidence is proof of their convictions. It's called "confirmation bias," also known as selective thinking, and defined as the inclination to notice and to look for those events that confirm one's beliefs while ignoring, undervaluing, or avoiding evidence that contradicts one's beliefs.

So how did hard science get in this New Age mess? "Motivational speakers glom onto quantum physics with thirty-two teeth because they see it as an opportunity [to advance their agenda]," says Fred Alan Wolf. Science has an air of the irrefutable about it. It's hard to argue with empirical-sounding data (even when wrongly interpreted), especially when amazing discoveries about physics, the brain, and biology are being made at a rapid pace.

Yet as many new unknowns have been discovered as new knowns. Unknowns open up a lot of maybes, which law of attraction supporters find very appealing. Even Harvard psychologist Ellen Langer is surprised when I tell her that some physicists, for example, dismiss the idea that "thoughts become things." "First-rate minds should be true to their discipline and say 'Who knows?'" she says. The problem is, however, that once "Who knows?" enters into the popular vernacular, it is very easy to transform "It *could* be true," and even "It's probably *not* true," into "It *is* true."

Physics for Simpletons

Physics's appeal to the spiritual world as a way of explaining the law of attraction and other mystical ideas is threefold. First, there is a debate raging among physicists about whether their discipline can explain human consciousness and reality. Second, the concepts and language of physics are at once inscrutable and very seductive, and therefore easily misconstrued, misunderstood, and misused by all sorts of people, including physicists. "When physicists write for the general public they have to oversimplify. You have to use metaphors, and your lay public does not realize they are analogies meant to communicate some fraction of what is going on. Popularization leads to mistranslation," says New York University physicist Alan Sokal.

The widespread use of quantum physics to prove supernatural phenomena exist is the direct result of a path the science has taken from the laboratory to the humanities departments of universities and into the hands of spiritual interpreters and mainstream laypeople who, many physicists says, have absolutely no idea what they are talking about—as least as far as science is concerned. For instance, the basic premise of the law of attraction—that like attracts like and thoughts are magnetic forces that draw thoughts on a similar frequency—is not entirely supported by science, which tells us that like electrical charges repel, and unlike electrical charges attract. Magnets repel each other. In other words, *opposites attract.* The prolific physicist Victor J. Stenger was so alarmed by the New Age tendency to take the term "quantum" out of its original scientific context, he wrote a book about its misuse called *The Unconscious Quantum: Metaphysics in Modern Physics and Cosmology* (1995). He critically appraises *Secret*-style metaphysical fads and argues that mystical notions say more about our fundamental need to believe than about the elemental makeup of the universe.

THE CONSCIOUSNESS CONUNDRUM

"It's partly my fault," replies *Secret* participant and physicist Fred Alan Wolf, "along with Gary Zukav and Fritjof Capra," when asked why the spiritual world has embraced science and particularly quantum physics. He was referring to his book, *Taking the Quantum Leap* (1981) and the books of two other physicists, which all delve into the relationship between quantum physics, consciousness, religion, and the mystical.

Zukav's *The Dancing Wu Li Masters* (1979) and Capra's *The Tao of Physics: An Exploration of the Parallels Between Modern Physics and Eastern Mysticism* (1975) were both mainstream bestsellers when they were published, and ushered in the now-popular trend of connecting quantum physics to how the mind "constructs" reality (it's all in your head) and Eastern religion. In the newest edition of his National Book Award–winning *Taking the Quantum Leap,* Wolf writes, "We are beginning a new age of awareness, the age of quantum consciousness, the age of the conscious atom."

The disagreements over consciousness and its relationship to quantum physics have been going on for decades. Robert B. Griffiths, a professor of physics at Carnegie Mellon University in Pittsburgh, Pennsylvania, says, "There is a public image that sees all scientists as being in agreement, but if you are on the inside you see there are disagreements and, depending on the topic, they can be wide or narrow." The consciousness debate isn't the only one going on in physics (the validity of string theory is also hotly contested). "Obviously there are aspects of physics that have confused the community for eighty years," Griffiths continues, "and given these confusing points it is a temptation to say that if the physicist does not understand it properly then I can say anything I want, and anything goes."

Professor Griffiths, author of *Consistent Quantum Theory* (2003), does not believe that quantum mechanics tells us anything about consciousness. "Having said that," he explains, "there are serious scientists, Roger Penrose among them, who claim the opposite. Those of us who do not accept it think Penrose has not made a cogent argument and we think there are good arguments on the other side."

Griffiths is referring to ideas Penrose outlined in *The Emperor's New Mind: Concerning Computers, Minds, and the Laws of Physics* (1989) and *Shadows of the Mind: A Search for the Missing Science of Consciousness* (1994). In those books, Penrose speculates that quantum mechanics plays a role in understanding human consciousness in that the microtubules within neurons, the structural components found in cells that are involved in many cellular processes—stay with me here—are part of the essential hardware the brain uses to do quantum computations—computations that computers cannot do.

Lee Spector, a professor of computer science in the School of Cognitive Science at Hampshire College, and one of the most respected authorities on artificial intelligence (AI) in the country, says that Penrose is a brilliant man who has made important contributions to the mathematics of physics, but who gets some things wrong when it comes to cognitive science, AI, and computers. "Penrose is completely right about the things that digital computers cannot do. There are incomputable problems, like the halting problem or the fact that it is impossible to write a program that can always accurately predict when another computer program will stop or when it will get stuck in a loop or continue running into infinity."

Penrose spends a lot of time on the significance of the halting problem, and, according to Spector (and others), tries to get people to believe that since humans can solve problems that digital computers can't, consciousness must therefore have something to do with quantum mechanics. "This is a fundamental mistake—the assumption that humans can solve problems that computers can't is wrong," says Spector. "But if you are with him that a human mathematician can solve incomputable problems, then you need some magic to explain it, so he reached for quantum mechanics because it seems magical."

The world-renowned mathematician Stephen Hawking has the same disagreement with Penrose, a position he described in a book Penrose himself wrote and edited. In *The Large, The Small, and the Human Mind* (1997), Hawking outlines his disagreements:

> Roger believes that consciousness is something special to living beings and that it couldn't be simulated on a computer. He didn't make it clear how objective reduction could account for consciousness. Rather, his argument seems to be that consciousness is a mystery and quantum gravity is another mystery so they must be related. Personally, I get a little uneasy when people, especially theoretical physicists, talk about consciousness.

"Henry Stapp at Berkeley is also quite wrong, but again, he is a serious man," says Griffiths. Stapp believes in something called quantum collapse, sometimes referred to as the "spiritual interpretation" of physics, which centers on the fact that observation of quantum experiments by a conscious observer is responsible for the wave-function collapse, another concept whose existence is also debated. The idea is related to the nineteenth-century New Thought idea that all is connected to the universe and we cannot be separated from everything that is going on in the world and in the cosmos. It aligns with Eastern philosophy, which says basically the same things. It's not hard to see how these ideas could lead some people to think that thoughts create things.

Stapp's position on quantum physics as related to reality, the mind, and consciousness is most directly described in the following quotes from his article "Why Classical Mechanics Cannot

Naturally Accommodate Consciousness but Quantum Mechanics Can" (psyche.cs.monash.edu.au/v2/psyche-2-05-stapp.html). Law of attraction believers use and reinterpret this kind of reasoning as proof that our thoughts create reality; therefore our thoughts create things. (Italics are mine.)

> *The physical body of the person and the surrounding world are represented by patterns of neural firings in the brain:* these patterns contain the information about the positioning of the body in its environment. They are represented in the context of neural templates for impending action. *The body-world schema has an extension that represents beliefs and other idea-like structures.*
>
> There is nothing within classical physics that provides for two such levels or qualities of existence or beingness, one pertaining to persisting local entities that evolve according to local mathematical laws, and one pertaining to sudden comings-into-beingness, at a different level or quality of existence, of entities that are bonded wholes whose components are the local entities of the lower-level reality. *Yet this is exactly what is provided by quantum mechanics, which thereby provides a logical framework that is perfectly suited to describe the two intertwined aspects of the mind/brain system.*

Like Griffiths, Lee Spector thinks this logic is flawed. "In quantum mechanics, observation or observability somehow does change experimental outcomes," he says, referring to the genuinely puzzling phenomenon that the scientist's observation (on an atomic scale) of an experiment makes a difference. However, this odd phenomenon is being spun to falsely reflect that *human consciousness* alters results in areas of life outside of the laboratory. "There has been a lot of discussion since the 1920s about how consciousness impacts the experiment, and there is a germ of truth there, but it does not apply to outcomes in the macroscopic [our] world," says Spector. Fred Alan Wolf says the same thing of physicists in *Taking the Quantum Leap:* "Now, much of what we observe is not at all disturbed or affected by observation."

Spector uses a simple example to illustrate his point. "You cannot influence how a randomly tossed coin is going to land by thinking about it or observing it fall. Observation in quantum physics is an interesting fact, but it does not say by thinking thoughts you can make certain things happen, even on a microscopic level. At any rate, even in quantum experiments, you cannot change or control the outcome *to what you want it to be* by observing it or being conscious of it." (Italics are mine.)

Byrne makes a passing reference to the thoughts of "great minds" of everyone from industrialist Andrew Carnegie to William Shakespeare to the Indian spiritual leader Krishnamurti paralleling the work of quantum physics. Carnegie and Shakespeare do not seem to have a direct connection to physics (see Part III for more on these two), but Krishnamurti does. And it's that connection, which no physicist I talked to mentioned, that might explain why law of attraction believers cling so tightly to the notion that quantum physics makes it so. David Bohm, who is not mentioned in *The Secret,* was an American quantum physicist who made numerous contributions to quantum theory, the philosophy of physics, and, indirectly, the Manhattan Project— the development of the atom bomb. Bohm was also involved in radical and communist politics. At any rate, Bohm found one of the Indian philosopher's books in 1959, and he saw similarities between what was in the book and his ideas about quantum mechanics. The two men even met, and became friends.

"Bohm is an interesting character," says Alan Sokal. "There are three Bohms, really. During his first period, until 1951, he was doing orthodox quantum mechanics; then, in 1952, he wrote an extremely interesting and heretical article in *Physical Review* that proposed a novel interpretation making quantum mechanics more like classical physics. For a long time the ideas in his article were not taken seriously, but now it is being debated. Then, later in his life, he became more New Agey and was friendly with various spiritual types, and his later books are in this vein. However, the New Age people are probably not familiar with his early work, which he never disavowed. He thought he was continuing the work he was doing in 1952."

A passage in Bohm's book, *Thought as a System,* might actually explain why spiritual people think quantum physics is such an important part of the law of attraction's validity.

What I mean by "thought" is the whole thing—thought, "felt," the body, the whole society sharing thoughts—it's all one process. It is essential for me not to break that up, because it's all one process; somebody else's thoughts becomes my thoughts, and vice versa. Therefore it would be wrong and misleading to break it up into my thoughts, your thoughts, my feelings, these feelings, those feelings.... I would say that thought makes what is often called in modern language a system. A system means a set of connected things or parts. But the way people commonly use the word nowadays it means something all of whose parts are mutually interdependent—not only for their mutual action, but for their meaning and for their existence.... Thought is constantly creating problems that way and then trying to solve them. But as it tries to solve them it makes it worse because it doesn't notice that it's creating them, and the more it thinks, the more problems it creates.

To be certain, the ideas of physics, and the disagreements among scientists, are much greater and more complicated than what I have laid out here, but even those physicists seem to agree that the science, including Bohm's interpretations, so far, does not indicate that we can conjure up cars, cash, jewelry, sexy girlfriends, or hunky husbands simply by thinking about them.

WORDS ARE THINGS

The first sentence of physicist Gary Zukav's popular book *The Dancing Wu Li Masters* explains a lot about why quantum physics is an appealing subject for the spiritual world to use in defending its positions on matters of attraction: "When I tell my friends I study physics, they move their heads from side to side, they shake their hands at the wrist, and they whistle, 'Whew. That's Difficult.'" Too difficult for the layman to argue with, and therefore easier for them to simply accept or get breathtakingly wrong.

Robert Griffiths notes that "even Nobel laureates [in physics] have gone on to say they do not understand aspects of quantum mechanics. The most blunt assertion came from Richard Feynman, who said no one understands it, and you have to take him rather seriously." Feynman, who died in 1988, was a Nobel Prize–winning American physicist who developed a new way to understand the behavior of subatomic particles, among other things. He also assisted in the development of the atom bomb.

Fred Alan Wolf has been trying to address the communication problem between scientists and laypeople for his entire professional life. "There are seekers, people who have no idea what science is, who are so far apart from scientists that they are now speaking babble because science talks with language they cannot understand. When they listen to someone who is way beyond their level of understanding, their own language [and understanding] gets fractured."

The counterintuitive, "break all the rules" nature of physics and quantum theories that sound mysterious to average readers is also part of the appeal for the mystical world. Barry Sanders, the iCore professor of quantum information science and director of the Institute for Quantum Information Science at the University of Calgary, believes that it comes from the measurement paradox in physics that does not allow physicists to consistently acquire facts. "In science you are used to conducting experiments to get measurable results. With quantum physics we are not able to incorporate measurements, so that's what gets people [who are not physicists] excited.

"Freshmen passing through my class on their way to medical school do not ask questions about physics and spirituality, but it's a different story when I give a public lecture on the subject." Sanders describes one such talk given at the Big Rock Brewery in Calgary, which was particularly enjoyable because payment was made in beer. "There were about a hundred people there clutching articles about quantum physics and spirituality. The Deepak Chopras of the world take ideas from quantum physics and translate for the spiritual realm, but for me as a hard-core scientist, I don't do it. But I can see how pervasive the inspiration of quantum physics is. Laypeople are intrigued by the words we use to describe quantum mechanics. For example, 'vibrating energy.' Those are beautiful words," says Sanders, words that are easy to reinterpret into something mystical. "If you read translations of Chinese Taoist books you get this idea that chi [pronounced "chee"] is energy and then the interpreter sees that physics talks about energy. The laws we write down have nothing to do with the chi concept of energy, but that's where I think some of the connections are being made," he adds.

Griffiths says he too has misgivings over some of the language that is used in his own specialty, quantum information. "For example, 'teleportation' is portrayed as a magical means of moving things from here to there, and it is not that at all. The original choice of the word makes it sound like something spectacular is going on. Well, something interesting *is* going on, but it is the sort of thing that is easily misinterpreted."

Lee Spector says that when he gives seminars, the language he uses can make him sound like a mystic, particularly when he discusses Peter Shor's algorithm for factoring extremely large numbers. "We say that parts of one large calculation is done in 'different universes,' and when we run the algorism we 'split the computer into many different versions of itself' that 'operate in different, parallel universes' and then we get them to come back and 'communicate in our universe.' There are physicists that take this literally. But maybe if you could observe it it would be happening in just one universe."

Griffiths says it is disappointing that the meaning of physics is distorted because of the language. "But there hasn't been a time when technical stuff wasn't misused by popular culture," he says. As an example, Griffith points out that Darwin's discoveries were turned into social Darwinism, creating, among other things, the justification for employers to oppress their workers. "So all sorts of misuses of concepts have gone through all time, and so we should not be too shocked by it, although in my opinion you should combat it when it happens," he says.

QUANTUM QUACKERY

The term "quantum quackery" was coined to criticize the trend of academics who are not scientists, but are mainly in the humanities, using quantum mechanics theories that they do not understand as scholarly sounding proof of any claim they care to make about anything and everything under the sun—from politics and gender bias to, well, the law of attraction. Quantum quackery was famously put to the test by Alan Sokal, a physics professor at New York University. Knowing about the so-called Sokal Affair is crucial to understanding the scientific claims related to *The Secret*. In 1996, Professor Sokal submitted a paper titled "Transgressing the Boundaries: Towards a Transformative Hermeneutics of Quantum Gravity" to the postmodern cultural studies periodical *Social Text,* a journal that was more popular among my peers than *People* magazine was when I was at Columbia graduate school in the 1980s. At the time articles in *Social Text* were not peer-reviewed; that is, the articles were not read for accuracy by other experts in the field before they were accepted for publication. (Peer review is accepted common practice at scientific and other academic journals.) Anyway, the article was a hoax filled with lots of postmodern lingo, scientific-sounding theories, and a far-left bias that Sokal knew the magazine would find appealing.

Sokal's aim was to find out if *Social Text* would publish the article, which was "liberally salted with nonsense if (a) it sounded good and (b) it flattered the editors' ideological preconceptions." His intention was realized. *Social Text* published the article in an issue devoted to the "Science Wars"—an argument between academic postmodernists and pragmatists about the nature of science. Sokal simultaneously published an article in a another journal, *Lingua Franca,* that exposed what he had done, describing his quantum article as a collection of absurd quotes about math and physics made by humanities scholars. The path quantum physics has taken from humanities scholars to New Age inspirational speakers seems almost inevitable. You can read Sokal's two papers, and more about his experiment, on his NYU Web page: www.physics.nyu.edu/faculty/sokal/.

Inspirational speaker John Demartini's assessment of quantum physics is a good example of how mainstreaming difficult concepts can get very mixed up. During an interview he told me this.

In quantum physics a particle of quantum or energy could be a particle of light. We call them gamma rays or radio waves. That little quantum can be separated in a cloud chamber and split into positrons and negatrons. If you put them together you return to light. Maybe consciousness is charged particles of light. Maybe consciousness is charged light in an unconditional way. We have radios waves that can send signals across the world in one-fourteenth of a second. Our thoughts are stored information in quantum waves.

Our consciousness can never be positive without negative, but our consciousness can think that it is true. We can separate the inseparable, but in actuality there is nothing but a quantum event. In quantum physics anytime you separate a quantum into two, the two parts are still entangled. If you alter one part, you alter the other instantaneously, which gave rise to faster than light particles. Once you do this, people [you are entangled with] are impacted wherever they are in the world. So anybody we have emotion about we are entangled with, so everything you see in them is represented in a part of yourself you are denying, and because they represent it, when you embrace it in them there is a quantum relationship—because it actually impacts them instantaneously, wherever they are.

First of all, physicist Fred Alan Wolf says you cannot fracture quantum into smaller quantum. "He is talking about the process where a photon of light can transform into a positron and electron but it is *not* a split. The quantum has changed form," says Wolf. Demartini is also talking about the idea of entanglement as it relates to human beings. In physics this is when the quantum states of two or more objects have to be described with reference to each other, even though the individual objects may be spatially separated. "I can tell you that in terms of people, entanglement in the sense that physicists talk about it is probably not true," says Wolf. "For example, my wife and I are very connected. We may be thinking the same thing sometimes, but just because I think of something bad does not mean my wife will experience something bad. It's just a fact—two people who are separated cannot influence the other with thoughts."

Alan Sokal uses simple logic to explain why it is dubious to believe human consciousness created the universe: "For most of the history of the universe humans have not existed. So it would be very weird if human consciousness played a part in its history or creation."

The Brain and Its Uses

The idea that our thoughts can change and mold outcomes in the world outside of ourselves begs a brief discussion of what the brain can and can't do. It turns out that what our brains are capable of is profound and awe inspiring—so incredible, in fact, that you would think that we wouldn't need to ascribe other supernatural powers to it. Here is a short assignment to do while you are reading: notice how the recent findings I describe, and expert's comments on them, could be easily misconstrued by people who desperately want to believe that science says we can change the world with our thoughts alone. None of the experts or authors quoted in this section believes this is true.

Advances in the understanding of neuroplasticity, or the brain's ability at the level of the neuron, to recover structurally or functionally after injury or disease, has made great strides in recent years. Two books on this exciting subject have been published recently. One by *Newsweek* science writer Sharon Begley, *Train Your Mind, Change Your Brain: How a New Science Reveals Our Extraordinary Potential to Transform Ourselves* (2007) and the other, *The Brain That Changes Itself: Stories of Personal Triumph from the Frontiers of Brain Science* (2007), by Norman Doidge, a research faculty member of the Columbia University Center for Psychoanalytic Training and Research and the University of Toronto Department of Psychiatry.

Begley looks at changes in the long-held theory that neurons in the brain don't regenerate. Her book carefully and accessibly describes a series of credible, carefully conducted experiments that show how new neurons are created in the brain every day, even in elderly people, something that until recently was not thought to be possible. With frequent tangents into Buddhist philosophy, Begley surveys current knowledge of neuroplasticity. Here is where metaphysical philosophers will descend: Begley discusses a series of experiments with Buddhists who have spent over ten thousand hours meditating that show it might be possible to train the brain to better experience emotions like compassion.

In the book, Begley describes how eighteen people practiced nonreferential compassion meditation that focuses the meditator on "unlimited compassion and loving-kindness toward all human beings." One kind of brain waves, gamma waves, grew exceptionally strong in the experienced meditators, the Buddhists. The gamma waves got a little stronger in the less experienced members of the test group. The Buddhists' gamma waves died down when they stopped meditating and went back up when they started again. This led researchers to conclude that the conscious or mindful thought, or brain training, can "create an enduring brain trait." Uh-oh. Can you see the misinterpretations coming around the corner?

"I repeat the caveat that what I know about *The Secret* is what I have read about it in *Newsweek*," says Begley, "and based on my understanding it says you can affect things in the outside world by the thoughts you think and there is not a plausible physical mechanism for that to happen. There is no commonality between that idea and neuroplasticity, which looks at patterns of thoughts and experiences that reach the brain through sensory organs and that can act back on the brain that received them. There is nothing spooky about it."

The aspect that is interesting about the thing we call the mind, explains Begley, is that the products of the brain can act back on the physical things that produced them with effects ranging from activity patterns to structural changes—but it's all based in very conventional physics. These discoveries have real medical significance. "In some mental disorders such as depression, stroke, and obsessive-compulsive disorder (OCD), something has gone wrong in the brain. People who have suffered stroke can expand the healthy areas of their brains in order to take on new jobs previously done by areas of the brain that were damaged. In the case of OCD, the biggest problem has been excessive worry; always thinking something has gone horribly wrong. Experiments at UCLA have shown that mindfulness meditation can decrease activity in the brain's worry circuit in the same way that SSR antidepressants [like Prozac] do," she says.

Begley says that part of mindful meditation's effectiveness has to do with thinking of yourself in the third person. In the OCD patient, the thought "I left the stove on" can disrupt an entire day with worry and fear. OCD patients can train their brain to view that thought as an "error message" that has nothing to do with reality: "Oh, that's my OCD talking." With practice, they are able to decrease brain activity related to worry in a therapeutic way.

"You could trace how thoughts manifest themselves at the level of electrical activity in the brain, and in this case it is acting back on activity in the worry circuit to interrupt it," explains Begley.

None of this, however, has any application to how thoughts and feelings can form something outside the brain, says Begley. "Positive thinking, yes, it can certainly impact ideas about personal competency, but not when it is a matter of turning the tides of the earth, literally. Thoughts, our brains, cannot do that," she says.

Recent discoveries about the changing brain have many implications for healthy people, says Norman Doidge. "The brain in certain respects is, indeed like a muscle insofar as it responds to exercise, and we can preserve or develop our brains with the proper exercise, and even strengthen weakened areas we thought we couldn't."

There is also some medical evidence that suggests that a high degree of stress is very bad for our brains and health. It is important to point out that stress from traumatic experience is what we are talking about, not "negative" thoughts, but painful or scary memories. Research done by J. Douglas Bremner, an associate professor of psychiatry and radiology at Emory School of Medicine and the author of *Does Stress Damage the Brain?*, has identified how severe psychological stress can affect brain structure and function.

"About 15 percent of people who are exposed to trauma will develop post-traumatic stress disorder, or PTSD, but 85 percent don't," says Bremner. According to him, people who are resilient to trauma are generally optimistic, so researchers try to measure resiliency and adaptive coping mechanisms to see how they can be adapted (or learned) by the 15 percent. There are common factors or traits that the 85 percent who can cope with trauma share: altruism, thinking and caring about others, and a sense of meaning and purpose in life. "For example, the prisoners of war in

Vietnam who naturally held beliefs that their country was a higher power, and those who believed in justice, faired better than those who did not," Bremner says.

One such man described how, during his captivity, he would visualize a pyramid with God, country, and family at the top, and this helped him survive without experiencing PTSD. The application value for understanding how resilient people think, says Bremner, is that research into the brains of resilient people can tell scientists how those who are not resilient can learn to retrain their brain to cope with or put their bad memories into perspective, and it goes way beyond positive thinking.

Norman Doidge explains it this way: "Think of the Vietnam vet who hears a car backfire, and who thinks he is back in Vietnam hearing gunfire. In treatment we don't so much 'eliminate' the memories as we turn the traumatic experience, which seems to be locked in the eternal present, into real memories, so the person can say, 'That is a memory, and it is over now. I can finally relax.'"

The Biology of Belief—Really

The idea that magical thinking might be part of our brain chemistry or makeup—that it is hard-wired into us for survival's sake—goes far in helping to explain the universal propensity for people to believe in supernatural phenomenon and "higher powers." SUNY Buffalo anthropology professor Phillips Stevens, Jr., says it is no surprise that so many people, from highly educated people living in technologically advanced countries, to those from impoverished areas of the world, believe in the magical powers of positive thinking.

"I first encountered this irrational optimism in the early 1960s as a Peace Corps secondary school teacher in Nigeria," he wrote to me in an e-mail, "in several frustrating cases of failing students' apparent refusal to acknowledge their situation. Even then, successful graduates faced overwhelming odds. Everyone knew the grim statistics: the schools and universities graduated thousands every year, but few would find employment in the modern sector. Yet every single school-leaver reflexively voiced a statement like: 'I will succeed,' or 'God will provide.' It is magical thinking, deriving from a probably universal human sense that people are interconnected with the cosmos, and that their thoughts and actions have direct influence on their environment and their future."

The adaptation of this belief has an invaluable practical advantage, says Stevens. "People know the facts and the odds, and they know that magic might not work; but they know that magic is easy and inexpensive and that it does work sometimes—and they know that cheer is an antidote to misery, and that negative thinking will make a bad situation worse."

So, the secret of *The Secret,* suggests Stevens, who has published numerous scholarly articles about the anthropology of magical thinking, "is our fundamental humanity. It might come out of evolutionary biology and evolutionary psychology." As for the popularity of magical thinking in Western society, Stevens says that it's appealing because it gives individuals a sense of control and self-importance in an increasingly confusing and impersonal world.

In his article "Magical Thinking in Complementary and Alternative Medicine," published in the November 2001 issue of *Skeptical Inquirer,* Stevens outlined five beliefs common to all forms of magical thinking found all the way back into prehistoric times—whether it is the law of attraction, positive thinking, or belief in special objects or colors. These five beliefs are forces of nature, energy and mystical power, interconnected cosmos, the power of symbols and words, and causality. "It is part of the way the human mind thinks, which is a biological process. In that sense, magical thinking makes sense," Stevens told me. In other words, if we did not believe in something bigger than ourselves, it may be hard to make meaning from our lives. But that does not make those beliefs true.

Seek and Ye Shall Find

Science, it seems, does not say our thoughts change the world outside of our own brains and our own perceptions. It does not say we attract things to us by our thoughts. The response made by some believers to these statements is often a knowing smile or a smirk of privileged information and understanding that implies, "The scientist who disagrees with us is merely frightened. He or she is fighting a scary fact they cannot admit to because of their own prejudices. Our knowledge is higher."

Such unwavering confidence is not easy to contend with, and not all believers take this "no debate" attitude. Some do see science and physics as a metaphor for the law of attraction, and not as actual proof (although most I have talked to say that physics offers literal proof). They may say things like: "People used to think the world was flat, so therefore, it is possible that we can move objects with our minds." Or: "No one believed Candace Beebe Pert, the neuroscientist, when she discovered the opiate receptors in the brain, so therefore it is possible for thoughts to attract things."

So please, don't take my word for it, read the original works of those credible sources quoted and referred to in this chapter, along with other believable sources working in the sciences in the "Further Reading" section of this book. Reading about science from reliable sources takes an intellectual commitment—another reason why many people are more prone to believe in magic. It's so much less time and thought consuming.

· 6 ·

The Bible and the Buddha:
Religious Roots of the Secret

RHONDA BYRNE SAYS the message of *The Secret* is buried within
the world's greatest religions: Hinduism, Hermetic traditions, Buddhism, Judaism, Christianity, and Islam. The connection seems
tenuous and limited to the idea that God supplies man with what
he needs—although most traditional theologians would say that
this is meant in terms of spiritual nourishment and strength to
deal with life's inequities and tragedies. While most of the great religions do not prohibit or even discourage men and women from
seeking success, the idea that peace of mind and happiness is found
in material goods and money is overwhelmingly rejected. In *God
in Search of Man: A Philosophy of Judaism* (1955), Rabbi Abraham
Joshua Heschel, the preeminent Jewish theologian of the twentieth
century, put this idea into brilliant perspective when he wrote:

> Dazzled by the brilliant achievements of the intellect in sci-
> ence and technique, we have not only become convinced

that we are the masters of the earth; we have become convinced that our needs and interests are the ultimate standard of what is right and wrong.

Comfort, luxuries, success, continually bait our appetites, impairing our vision of that which is required but not always desired. They make it easy for us to grow blind to values. Interests are the value-blind man's dog, his pathfinder and guide.

While a complete survey of world religions is not the purpose of this chapter, it is possible to draw conclusions about whether or not the law of attraction is supported across religions, specifically in the way it is presented in *The Secret:* as a way to attain material happiness and conventional definitions of worldly success. Because of space constraints I limit the inquiry to Christianity, Judaism, Buddhism, and another religion, one that Byrne seems to almost purposely avoid mentioning, Christian Science, an offshoot of the New Thought movement and the doctrine most closely aligned with *The Secret* and the law of attraction philosophy.

Sociology professor Darren Sherkat says that connecting *The Secret* to religion is a very successful strategy because it gives it a sense of legitimacy. "For those who are connected to a specific religion, it will not be a crossover book because they go to the Christian or Pentecostal businessman's prayer meeting and have their own booksellers and ministers who tailor success talk to the denomination, but for people who are not located within a specific religion, and who often dabble within traditions, anything that seems universal across religions is extremely appealing and reassuring."

Instead of worshiping a higher power, God, Jesus, or Mohammad, *The Secret* believer worships his or her own power and that of the universe. Reports of people watching the movie multiple times are common. Several news stories reported people watching the film thirty-five times or listening to *The Secret* CD to and from work every day for weeks on end, as if the watching and the listening imbued them with the power of attraction. This is very similar to classic forms of religious worship, where repetition of prayer and study of sacred texts, like the Bible or the Koran, is common. Treating the DVD, the book, and the CD as material objects of power is fetishistic too. The word "fetish" derives from the Latin *factitius,* meaning "to do or make." Most experts agree that the word was probably first used to describe handmade idols and amulets that were thought to be imbued with magical properties. In today's world, the shiny round DVD and CD disc and the slickly packaged book become the contemporary believer's totem.

MIT media professor Henry Jenkins says it's not surprising that people watch, read, or listen to *The Secret* multiple times as part of their law of attraction devotion or practice. "There are a handful of media genres that people watch over and over again: exercise, porn, children's material, and Christian or religious programs," he says. "The kind of work you watch fifteen times is structured differently from those that you watch once, such as a narrative film. There is a sense in these other categories that you haven't gotten it all and you have to keep watching to find what you missed. Watching again and again may yield emotional insights, and enable the reader (or viewer) to grasp and pass along the important meaning embedded in the words (or images)."

Jenkins has studied the way the religious communities, particularly Christians, have adapted themselves to fan culture, and embraced what he calls "transmedia narratives"—stories that spread across multiple media platforms—and fan activities to help build a fellowship.

Working through information repeatedly, meditating and reflecting on it, and praying over it is what gives the work, in this case *The Secret,* scriptural power, says Jenkins. "My grandfather had a third-grade education and he read the Bible six times in his life, which is an incredible accomplishment in literacy." *The Secret* is a fraction of the size of the Bible in both words and meaning, and therefore much easier to read and reread. "There is not a lot there, but the words speak spiritual truths and many people have been transformed by them," Jenkins observes. The book also allows many secular people, or those who are turned off by organized religion, to find a spiritual truth without having to consider the moral constraints that traditional faith requires.

"At the current moment, there is more and more spiritual work that is touching nonbelievers, so the sense of religious conversation extends outward from an evangelical setting to a larger public that looks for something that can help them deal with modern life," says Jenkins, who points to the popularity of evangelical preacher Rick Warren's *The Purpose Driven Life* among nonevangelicals. "Warren is one of those writers who has not buried the Bible in his work, but I keep hearing about him from nonbelievers who find his book deeply meaningful, so he has found a language to speak outside of Christianity."

While the premise of "ask, believe, receive" is somewhat universal across religions, *The Secret*'s interpretation reverses it. It is a common magical theme, but here you are not talking about receiving blessings in the afterlife, says sociology professor Darren E. Sherkat. "Instead it talks about how otherworldly things will get you worldly goods. Rather than addressing how your worldly stuff determines your afterlife, this is about getting the stuff for your life."

Sherkat echoes the view of many in traditional faith communities when he says this materialistic view is dangerous and rejected by most established religious groups. "They understand it is not going to work out in the long run because a few people will get something, but most people won't," he explains. That imbalance makes it a very shallow religion for the majority of people, who are not going to attain the success and acquisitions they are hoping for. Sherkat explains that when you promise people that faith alone will get them something material in the here and now, they can empirically verify it, and therefore refute it easily when things don't work out. The danger of that is you can lose your flock when they become disillusioned with the false promise. Assuring riches in the afterlife, of course, is not provable or disprovable. "Successful Christian groups don't make definitive promises," according to Sherkat.

The theology of success, as Sherkat called it, is very common in conservative Christian denominations, both Protestant and Catholic, and particularly in many poor African American congregations. "You see a lot of preaching to those who are less inclined to succeed, so it may be comforting to do it for a couple of years, but then you realize after three or four years that you are still an underpaid administrative assistant and it becomes very superficial. Especially when you have been giving money to a rich preacher in a white suit, driving a Rolls-Royce. It's all fine and dandy for CEOs, but it is not really good for lower-level and midmanagement people whose jobs are on the line," says Sherkat.

Another problem that arises in the all-or-nothing quality you need to believe in the law of attraction is the sense of guilt that comes when things don't work out as anticipated. "It is very dangerous for an established religion to dabble in magic, whether it's saying congregants can be rich or healed of disease," says Sherkat. The sociology professor recounts an experience a woman he knew had with a minister at an Assembly of God church. "He told her that the reason her husband died of cancer was because he did not have enough faith. She didn't buy it, because he was a good guy by all the standards of his faith. For the minister to impugn the person's faith and potentially undermine their family is dangerous. They became outraged and complained, and he was thrown out." But, the minister went on to found another successful denomination.

Christian Attraction

While Byrne acknowledges other religions, there is a strong Christian flavor to *The Secret*'s ask, believe, receive idea, albeit a highly interpretative one tailored to suit the materialism of the modern Western world. Absent from it are pesky concepts like sacrifice, charity, and brotherhood. Jenkins says that the mainstreaming of Christianity, which some call secularization, serves a purpose that not everyone in the Christian world agrees with. "When Christian rock artists go mainstream, they often mask their message. Some say it broadens the message, and others think the message is corrupted. There is a deep debate about it within the fundamentalist world, because some see the materialism of pop culture as antithetical to Christian values." On the other hand, Jenkins says, Christians have always been adept at embracing new mediums to market their beliefs and pop culture allows them to use various mediums to create new, young fans for Jesus.

Some are bothered by the lack of credit Byrne gives to the Bible, which might have been done on purpose to, as Jenkins says, attract people who might otherwise be turned off by it. Dr. Ben Johnson, who contributed to both the DVD and the book, notes that "much of what it says, including many specific words, are almost direct quotes from the Bible, but no one gave that credit." Lime Radio's Laura Smith remarked on "how slow *The Secret* is to acknowledge Jesus. I got to page 40, and it had yet to quote Jesus." Indeed, it is not until page 47 that Byrne brings up the New Testament and ask, believe, receive, which she describes as the Bible's "three simple steps" for getting what you want. It's religion lite for the quasispiritual masses.

Not everyone sees *The Secret*'s interpretation of ask, believe, receive as benign or accurate. Oliver Thomas, a Southern Baptist minister and constitutional lawyer active in public debates about religion, science, and education, and author of *10 Things Your Minister Wants to Tell You: (But Can't, Because He Needs the Job)*, thinks *The Secret* has a very dark side. "It contains some of the most destructive theology to come down the pike in recent years," he wrote in an e-mail. "It sets up millions of gullible, yet innocent, people for disappointment, disillusionment, and guilt. It's not just bad theology. It's dangerous theology."

Thomas says Byrne takes New Testament theology out of context and morphs it into what he calls "prosperity theology." "She is not the first to do this, it's been all over TV for years. Lots of Christian televangelists have built empires on this line of thinking," he says. Yet most Christian theologians interpret "ask and you shall receive" to mean praying to or in Jesus' name not just in a perfunctory kind of way, but in the sense that you are aligning yourself with the same things that Christ would ask for or want in the world. "When we ask God to do something it is consistent with what God wants to occur on Earth, it is not a personal indulgence. He is not a cosmic Santa Claus," notes Thomas.

You can see that without theological instruction of careful reading the following passages from the Bible can easily be misunderstood.

> If ye abide in me, and my words abide in you, ye shall ask what ye will, and it shall be done unto you.
>
> JOHN 15:7

> Again I say unto you, That if two of you shall agree on earth as touching any thing that they shall ask, it shall be done for them of my Father which is in heaven.
>
> MATTHEW 18:19

> And I say unto you, Ask, and it shall be given you; seek, and ye shall find; knock, and it shall be opened unto you.
>
> LUKE 11:9

> Be careful for nothing; but in every thing by prayer and supplication with thanksgiving let your requests be made known unto God.
>
> PHILIPPIANS 4:6

For the traditional Christian, prayer is best understood as a moment to match personal intentions and thoughts with the will of God, according to Thomas. It should be consistent with the transcendent force in the universe. "When you pray like that they are going to be sacrificial," he says. Instead of asking for money, cars, houses, fame, or business success, you instead ask for assistance and strength for the things that life inevitably throws our way. For example, "God help me to have the strength to help my neighbor the way I should," "Help me to stand up for my gay classmate who is being ridiculed," or "Please give me the patience

I need to be a good nursemaid to my husband, who has Alzheimer's disease." That's what Jesus is talking about when he said, Ask and you shall receive, according to the pastor.

"It hurts when you see a book like this become so successful, not because the author is making money, that's the American way, after all, but having read the book, it is clear that the ideas in it can be harmful to innocent folks who are not theologically trained." This line, from Byrne's introduction, is the kind of promise that can fill a desperate person with hope, which can be devastatingly dashed in an instant: "It doesn't matter who you are or where you are, The Secret can give you whatever you want."

When people put their faith in their thoughts, what inevitably happens, says Thomas, is life's own agenda gets in the way. "God is not a grand master puppeteer controlling everything." The pastor points out that Christian scripture says the rain falls on the just and the unjust, and that God has imposed certain laws and constraints on his universe, and when things go wrong, it has nothing to do with whether you are good, bad, or indifferent. "Life is random. Good ministers do not set up false expectation among their congregants, and that's what's wrong with *The Secret*. It preaches you can be healthy and a billionaire by using law of attraction. The fact is, there are millions of Americans who would crash if they stopped taking their meds," he says. Or quit their jobs if they believed they could think themselves rich more easily sitting at home.

Unfortunately, Thomas says, a lot of Christian ministers preach this idea. "I was listening to Oral Roberts on TV, and he said something like, 'Now put your hands on the TV and believe that God can make a miracle for you.' And I envision all these little old ladies on fixed incomes doing that to help their bad backs, and then sending in their checks to the ministry."

Many Pentecostal ministers believe in literal healings, as does Thomas. However, the distinction he makes is that he does not know why it happens (whereas the Pentecostal may say it is the will of God; *The Secret* says it is a direct result of pure positive thought). "Doctors with a little gray in their hair will tell you they see such things happen, but the notion that healing comes only to those who have enough faith lands many people in despair and depression," he says. "There are any number of things in this weird life that are random and have nothing to do with our attitude."

Judaism: Intention and Transformation

Byrne says that the secret law of attraction is found in Judaism. But it seems doubtful that the teachings of the Talmud are meant for personal aggrandizement. Rabbi Geoffrey W. Dennis, the rabbi of Congregation Kol Ami in Flower Mound, Texas, and author of *Encyclopedia of Jewish Myth, Magic and Mysticism* (2007), says that there are fine, loose threads that connect the law of attraction to Judaism. He explains that the notion of *kavanah* in Jewish mysticism, which is bringing the right intention to your prayer and actions, brings honor to acts of Judaism, whether they are ritual or moral. "It has a cosmic power, God really wants us to be his partners in transforming the world," he says, "but this power is not intended for your own benefit."

Tikkun olam is another important term in this context, according to Rabbi Dennis. "It means mending the world or rectifying the world, if we take seriously the commission that God gives us. It is a paradox because we are small, weak cells with tremendous power to complete the work of creation." He draws distinctions with the success orientation in *The Secret*. "This is not a self-indulgent task, for personal gain or reward. The use of *kavanah,* intent, does not make us more handsome. Rather it is an extension of your love of God."

Positive thinking, or like attracts like, always has another, problematical, side, says Rabbi Dennis, who illustrates the dilemma with a story: "You are walking home and see the flames of a fire rising from your neighborhood. So you say to yourself, God, let the house that is on fire *not* be mine. One, the fire is already happening and you are asking God to change reality, and two, by asking that it not be your house, you are also asking that the fire be at a neighbor's house." Realistically and morally there are some things you probably should not expect of God.

Judaism does affirm the idea that everything happens for a purpose, and sometimes, says Dennis, it is hard for us to wrap our heads around that concept when it comes to tragedy and hardship. "But affirming there is a value in every experience allows us to conclude that there is meaning to life; isn't that worse than feeling there is no purpose to events?" he says. "If we look back through our life, we can see the fingerprints of God in our life. He is always revealed when we look backward."

We are empowered and have capacities that border on the divine, says Dennis, yet magically wishing or thinking things into being doesn't jibe with Judaism. The problem, he says, is that our mind is godlike, and we can imagine being godlike, and we can come very close, to doing anything and achieving anything. But the pathos of human experience means that we cannot always achieve everything we'd like to because we have limitations. "We have to balance the reality of our empowerment and our fate. There are certain things we have no control over. The reality is, we are all going to die, we all grow older, we all have to leave third grade, which was our favorite class. You know the [AA] saying, 'Grant me the serenity to accept the things I cannot change, the courage to change the things I can, and the wisdom to know the difference.'"

Twisting the Path of Buddhism

Byrne quotes Buddha's "All that we are is a result of what we have thought" to mean that thoughts create our reality and can attract things to us, good and bad. Rider University psychology professor John Suler notes that the spiritual connections between the law of attraction can be tenuously traced to the roots of Buddhism. "Some of the items in the Eightfold Path of Buddhism, the principles for finding a happy life, include 'right speech' and 'right thought'—which essentially amount to thinking and speaking in positive ways. It's the 'What goes around comes around' principle. If you think and speak in positive ways, if you send 'positive waves' out there into the world, then that's what you get in return," he explains.

Buddhism is one of the oldest religions practiced today, dating back to the third century B.C., when it was an obscure faith based on the philosophy of Siddharta Gautama (the Buddha), who renounced his life of luxury and instead ultimately embraced the idea of practicing a spirituality that studied and eventually led to insight into the true nature of life. Meditation is an important part of the Buddhist practice, specifically to develop favorable characteristics, such as awareness, kindness, and wisdom, which can culminate in enlightenment. It does not include the worship of a single creator or god, which is confusing for some people who may view it as a philosophy and not a religion. And many people who consider themselves a member of another traditional religion, such as Christianity and Judaism, practice Buddhist philosophy right alongside their other faith, with no feelings of conflict.

Richard Seager, associate professor of religious studies at Hamilton College, an expert in American Buddhism, and author of *Buddhism in America* and *Encountering the Dharma,* says that Buddhists do think a lot about the real-world benefits of their religion. Japanese versions of it, he says, have historically placed an emphasis on the proceeds that come from observance and practice. "The idea that if you are going to get involved in a religion, you do so because you are going to get something out of it, can be found everywhere in Japanese Buddhist groups. It works out of this general Japanese frame of reference that speaks to real needs of people who are suffering. If you are starving to death, you can chant for food; if you are out of a job, you can chant for employment," he explains.

When talking about Buddhist pragmatism or practicality, Seager points specifically to the Soka Gakkai movement, which promotes world peace and individual happiness based on the teachings of Mahayana Buddhism, which became very prevalent in Japan after World War II. "The dispossessed people of the country chanted for concrete things they needed to survive after the war. Believers always make a distinction between conspicuous or concrete and inconspicuous or spiritual benefits."

When the movement traveled West and coincided with what many people see as the rise of cultural narcissism in the United States, the emphasis on the material got distorted, and focused on conspicuous benefits that may not be necessities for life (like a job or food). "It goes to the lowest common denominator and becomes highly generalized, and ultimately indistinguishable from the New Thought movement," says Seager.

Another way to think of benefits in Buddhism, which may have a weak link to the law of attraction, is what Seager calls the noble truth that all life is suffering. "The flip side of that is

Buddhism says there is a way out of it; there are ways to find happiness," he says. And having good things come to you is related to karma. "Now if you are a philosophically minded person, happiness will take place on a spiritual plane or through inconspicuous benefit," Seager explains.

There is also a very broad range of sophisticated Buddhist philosophy that says the mind and the cosmos are connected—and this concept might be what Byrne is referring to when she says her Secret is found in Buddhism, according to Seager. He explains it this way: "In the broadest possible terms, for the Mahayana Buddhist, there is no distinction between the mind here and the universe out there because they partake of the same reality. I associate this view more with Chinese Buddhism, the idea that all life is a dream. However, this is an extreme position and I think the modern view puts more emphasis on fulfilling social needs."

Hands-On Religion

Christian Science, or the Church of Christ, Scientist, is a small Protestant denomination that practices Christian healing in a way that is meant to mirror healing performed by Jesus and his followers. According to Stephen Barrett, who runs the Web site Quackwatch, membership in the church has declined steadily over the past thirty years. Never especially large, in 1971 there were 1,829 churches; in 2005 there were just 1,010. The number of Christian Science practitioners (healers) and teachers has also declined severely from a 1971 high of 4,965 to a 2005 all-time low of 1,161. The greatest concentration of healers and teachers then and now is in California (1,246 and 259, respectively), perhaps because of population size. Massachusetts, where the mother church and *Christian Science Monitor* offices are located, boasts only 101 practitioners today; it had 295 back in 1971. Florida, Illinois, and New York lead the pack after California in terms of members.

Mary Baker Eddy founded the sect in 1879, and her book, *Science and Health with Key to the Scriptures,* is the fundamental text used by church members. As discussed in Chapter 4, Phineas Quimby, who is believed to be one of the originators of the New Thought movement, profoundly influenced Eddy's view of illness as an illusion when she met him first as a patient. Her view that sickness is a construct of the human mind, a position shared by Rhonda Byrne, was formed at that time.

After she fell on the street and hurt her back in 1866, Eddy medicated herself with Bible study, which she claimed cured her spinal injury (although historical records say she sued the city of Lynn, Massachusetts, because of lasting ill effects from her accident). She spent the rest of her life establishing a network of churches and reading rooms across the country. When she was eighty-seven she founded *The Christian Science Monitor,* a respected newspaper that is still published today.

The three basic tenets of Christian Science are, according to the church's Web site:

1. God is divine Love, Father-Mother, supreme.
2. The true nature of each individual as a child of God is spiritual.
3. God's infinite goodness, realized in prayer and action, heals.

Lime Radio director of programming Laura Smith says Christian Science was her original introduction to metaphysics; she learned about it from a pamphlet she found in New York's Grand Central Station. "It made a lot of sense to me. I am not in the church anymore, but I use its premise of the science of the metaphysics," she says. Christian Science's absence from *The Secret* doesn't surprise Smith, who says it was left out probably because so many people misunderstand it. "People always think, 'Oh, that's the religion that does not go to doctors; they practice spiritual healing,' and that turns people off."

Smith's assessment is not far off base, since Christian Science sees illness as an illusion that a practitioner can eliminate with healing prayer. "*The Secret*'s chapter on health reminds me of Christian Science," says Pastor Thomas. "Every once in a while I run into former Christian Scientists who have lost a child to a simple illness that could have been treated with a noninvasive antibiotic and it is horrific." *The Secret* does not take the idea of abandoning medicine quite as far as Christian Science does, but it does put forward the idea that if you have the right mental attitude you will have perfect health. "This plays into the health problems facing Americans" without offering any genuine help or useful advice, argues Thomas. "If I sit on the couch and think positive, I am never going to get to the gym. It runs counter to what good healthy living is about."

While health, mental and physical, is a centerpiece of Christian Science thought, there is no mention of the law of attraction per se in Eddy's *Science and Health,* although the following passage is related to the idea of like attracts like.

We weep because others weep, we yawn because they yawn, and we have smallpox because others have it; but mortal mind, not matter, contains and carries the infection. When this mental contagion is understood, we shall be more careful of our mental conditions, and we shall avoid loquacious tattling about disease, as we would avoid advocating crime. Neither sympathy nor society should ever tempt us to cherish error in any form, and certainly we should not be error's advocate.

As for the power of the mind, she writes:

> Christian Science explains all cause and effect as mental, not physical. It lifts the veil of mystery from Soul and body. It shows the scientific relation of man to God, disentangles the interlaced ambiguities of being, and sets free the imprisoned thought. In divine Science, the universe, including man, is spiritual, harmonious, and eternal. Science shows that what is termed matter is but the subjective state of what is termed by the author's mortal mind.

Eddy does not address "ask, believe, receive" and seems to take a dim view of human vanity and materialism:

> Beauty, wealth, or fame is incompetent to meet the demands of the affections, and should never weigh against the better claims of intellect, goodness, and virtue. Happiness is spiritual, born of Truth and Love. It is unselfish; therefore it cannot exist alone, but requires all mankind to share it.

Eddy issues a stern warning to those who use mental science for selfish reasons:

> The Science of mental practice is susceptible of no misuse. Selfishness does not appear in the practice of Truth or Christian Science. If mental practice is abused or is used in any way except to promote right thinking and doing, the

power to heal mentally will diminish, until the practitioner's healing ability is wholly lost.

The Secret's focus on the fulfillment of material dreams, which almost every organized religion, save the theology of Wall Street, rejects, might optimistically be viewed as a way of drawing people into a spiritual life, with the hope that fans will eventually be compelled to a higher purpose. Time will tell if that's true. It may be difficult for those people to make the leap. Sociologist Darren Sherkat says that when people realize that it doesn't work, many, especially those suffering from mild forms of mental illness, who he says are very attracted to miraculous-sounding cures, will gravitate toward other magical solutions. "Then the next moral entrepreneur can take the place of the one who has burned out his or her followers."

As for Baptist minister Oliver Thomas, who sees religion as something that should be life-affirming, not life-denying, the message of *The Secret* is problematical and may end up turning people off faith entirely if they become disillusioned with the book's spectacular promise. "It's pernicious, because on the surface it looks like it is life-affirming and joyful, but beneath the surface you see that it is pretending that life is something that it is not." Thomas is reminded of what both Dr. Albert Schweitzer and German Lutheran pastor Dietrich Bonhoeffer said about the high purpose of faith, which is in high-relief contrast to *The Secret*:

> Seek always to do some good, somewhere. Every man has to seek in his own way to realize his true worth. You must give some time to your fellow man. For remember, you don't live in a world all your own. Your brothers are here too.
> —Dr. Albert Schweitzer

Cheap grace is the deadly enemy of our Church. We are fighting to-day for costly grace. Cheap grace means grace sold on the market like cheapjacks' wares. The sacraments, the forgiveness of sin, and the consolations of religion are thrown away at cut prices. . . . The essence of grace, we suppose, is that the account has been paid in advance; and, because it has been paid, everything can be had for nothing.

—DIETRICH BONHOEFFER, *The Cost of Discipleship*

Part III

❧

GENIUSES,
PHILOSOPHERS,
MADMEN, AND
ROBBER BARONS—
DID THEY
REALLY KNOW
THE SECRET?

The Secret mentions many luminaries from various fields and times in connection with the law of attraction. Byrne says that people as diverse as Shakespeare, Emerson, Beethoven, and Henry Ford used it, even if they weren't actually aware of it. It is an intriguing notion—did Plato, Carl Jung, Robert Browning, Ralph Waldo Emerson, and Albert Einstein actually practice, even unwittingly, the law of attraction? Did they actively believe their thoughts became things? Was their success based on ask, believe, receive? Or is it that anyone who gains fame and fortune, whether from talent or industry, is by definition of their accomplishments using the law of attraction, no matter what they themselves believe? If that's the explanation that law of attraction believers would give—well, it may be pointless to look into the lives of these men. Byrne might say that anyone who has made anything important out of his or her life used the law of attraction to do so. The logic being that talent, money, fame, and success are *always* products of the law of attraction. But I am not sure this is true. I think leaving it at that diminishes the accomplishments (and shortcomings) of these men.

I have selected nine of the men Byrne mentions and investigated whether or not you could really say they had a driving law of attraction philosophy behind their success and creative or business endeavors. In the arts, the focus is on composer Ludwig van Beethoven, playwright William Shakespeare, and writer Ralph Waldo Emerson. Next, I look at three men who each in their own way had a huge impact on the twentieth century: Thomas Alva Edison, Winston Churchill, and Albert Einstein. From the business world, I chose Andrew Carnegie, William Clement Stone, and Henry Ford.

This section is not an attempt to write complete biographies of these people—there are many good life stories available about most, if not all, of these men. What I have tried to do is look at their lives through the law of attraction lens. Where might it have shown up in their stories and the way they lived their lives? How did it manifest itself—how *didn't* it?

There are certainly many valid philosophical discussions about whether talent is primarily nature or nurture, or more likely a combination of both. Practice makes perfect—both are essential to developing a natural talent into something extraordinary. Every one of the subjects in this section was a tireless *doer*—committed to his passion and ideas, even if they were a combination of genius and craziness, as seems to be the case with Henry Ford. Thought alone didn't earn these men the place in history they all enjoy.

Creative Types: Ludwig van Beethoven, William Shakespeare, and Ralph Waldo Emerson

ARTISTIC CREATIVITY. WHERE does it come from? Is it a trait that you're born with, a state shaped by nature and nurture, luck and pluck? Why are some talented people able to make something of their gifts while others, equally talented, find it difficult to win the attention and admiration of the public? Creative genius has an aura of mystery and magic because it differs from other cognitive activities, such as problem solving or the straightforward memorization of facts and figures. The intrinsic or essential quality of creativity makes it ripe for magical interpretations—and who knows? Genius does seem divine. Did Beethoven, Shakespeare, and Emerson look to the universe for inspiration? Did they believe that their abilities came *only* from the cosmos? There is an enormous body of work that analyzes the minds and work of these three greats—so attempting to answer those questions in this short space is not only not possible, it is inadvisable. However, if we take a brief look at their lives, and their own words, we can draw some conclusions about their philosophies vis-à-vis the law of attraction.

Beethoven: Love and Music

Beethoven is generally considered to be one of the greatest composers in the history of music. He was born in Bonn in 1770, moved to Vienna in 1792, and died in 1827 when he was just fifty-six. He showed musical promise when he was still a boy, and in a bout of positive thinking on his father's part, was encouraged, some say forced, to develop his skills as a pianist by practicing almost nonstop. His father had dreams of success and wealth for his son (and thus for himself), because he was well aware of the kind of fame and fortune musical talent had brought Mozart. As a professional musician, Beethoven was sought after as a solo pianist, and he also played the violin with both aptitude and artistry. By all accounts, he was a good neighbor, a loyal friend, and a lover of nature (he always took summer homes in the forests outside of Vienna) and looked at life as a universe of the possible.

The composer worked during a transitional period both in terms of musical form and society. He straddled the classical and romantic eras in music, with classical in this context meaning formal, ordered, and rational and romantic referring to emotional, more loosely structured, and sometimes explosive in expression. It was also the first time in history when musicians had to be freelancers instead of being part of the economic and social system of the court or church. Mozart was the first freelancer, but Beethoven was also one of the earliest composers who had to make his way as an independent contractor. Both men were still dependent on the royals and the aristocrats, who tended to treat Beethoven well. However, the composer resented the fact that he was not considered their equal; he could not, for example, marry a woman of the court.

Beethoven was popular among the cognoscenti, and several aristocrats got together and agreed to pay him a stipend so he could compose without having to worry about money for the bulk of his life. The fact that he was dependent on them proved a double-edged sword. On one hand, he was secure and free to write what he pleased. On the other, he had to put up with a class system he didn't really agree with. He didn't exactly bite the hands that fed him, but once when he was playing solo piano at an aristocratic soirée, he became irritated when some of the audience talked during his performance. He was famously said to have risen from his bench and announced, "There are many noblemen, but only one Beethoven."

His view of the world was a universal one, which was at odds with the rigid and unbreakable class distinctions of the day. The words to his Ninth Symphony, for example, express the idea that all men are brothers, a romantic sentiment very different from the prevailing view that men were defined by their birth rank. He was sympathetic with the French and American revolutions, and until Napoleon made himself emperor, Beethoven was actually a fan of the conqueror, thinking Napoleon would unify Europe and work for a democratic system. Consequently, Beethoven was deeply disappointed with his hero, going so far as to cut Napoleon's name out of his Third Symphony.

As far as the law of attraction, well, Beethoven believed both in the universality of man and in his own powers as a composer. *The Secret*'s Web site asserts that Beethoven was "considered to be a Rosicrucian," but it does not say by whom. I could not find any references to it in the six most respected biographies—including Thayer's *Life of Beethoven,* and those by Edmond Morris,

Maynard Solomon, Lewis Lockwood, Anton Felix Schindler, and Russell Martin. His urge to compose certainly must have begun with a "positive thought"—all creativity begins, and is ultimately sustained, that way. The focus of his life was music; it was the driving force that kept him from wallowing in very real shortcomings that might have stopped a lesser man.

Beethoven's growing deafness, coupled with the fact that he was rather small in stature, pockmarked, and not terribly attractive (and most likely suffered from less than pleasant hygiene), led him to retreat deeply into himself and his music, which eventually became his only means of communication. One could say he approached composition with an unwavering positivism and love. He understood that art could be a universal message that everyone could enjoy or be uplifted by, and he was the first composer to really express the full range of human emotion as the central theme of all his music. While his music is extremely powerful, it also enjoyed a wide appeal, which is what he wanted.

Beethoven was a principled man, according to Ignaz von Seyfried a friend and fellow musician. In 1832 von Seyfried wrote a book, *Beethovens Studien,* which is widely considered to be accurate in terms of its personal reminiscences of his friendship with the composer. His description of Beethoven certainly hints of a man who sought the same good behavior he expected of himself in his friends—this often meant he had trouble finding and maintaining close relationships. Von Seyfried wrote that justice, personal decency, a devout mind, and religious purity meant a great deal to Beethoven. "A man is as good as his word" was his motto, and friends understood that promises not kept resulted in his anger.

The composer may have reached higher states of consciousness through playing, writing, and listening to music. J. W. N.

Sullivan in *Beethoven: His Spiritual Development* (1927) writes about the composer's final quartets and says, "Beethoven had reached the state of consciousness that only the great mystics have ever reached, where there is no more discord. And in reaching it he retained the whole of his experience of life; he denied nothing." When Beethoven was just twenty-two, after moving from the local music scene in Bonn to the more prestigious and international stage of Vienna, Sullivan says the prodigy was well aware of his significant abilities and valued them highly: "When, in his early twenties, he went to Vienna it was with a courageous self-confidence commensurate with his power and originality, a self-confidence very necessary for the full safeguarding of that originality."

Beethoven's personal library was filled with a variety of historical and philosophical volumes, poetry, and works by writers of the day, some of whom he knew. His interest in the language of beauty would certainly give way to the idea that he had a positive view of man and nature. Many of the books had all the earmarks of being well and carefully read—sections marked with lead pencil, pages turned over to hold a place. According to his contemporary, Anton Felix Schindler, the *Odyssey* and its beautifully written stories of people, places, and adventure, "never ceased to delight him."

In *Beethoven As I Knew Him* (1860; translated and republished in 1966 and 1996), Schindler writes that Beethoven also had the complete works of Shakespeare and works by Goethe, as well as the poetry of Friedrich Schiller, Christoph August Tiedge, and other contemporaneous poets. The works of Plato, Aristotle, Plutarch, and Xenophon, Pliny, Euripides, Quintilian, Ovid, Horace, Ossian, Milton, and Thomson all had a place on his shelves, and ideas from these books can be found in his own diary entries and in letters to friends. A favorite book, one that has been lost to time, was Nina d'Aubigny von Engelbronner's *Briefe an Natalie uber den Gesang,* which was about the nature of singing.

Brought up as a Catholic, Beethoven formed an independent opinion of religion as a young man, doubtless as a result of coming of age during the Enlightenment. Beethoven's own words show that he was aware of the divine order of the universe, and that beauty and music were the result of a higher power. These passages are the best way to demonstrate Beethoven's worldview, which is more complicated than a simple interpretation of the law of attraction allows.

In 1816 he wrote in his diary: "It was not the fortuitous meeting of the chordal atoms that made the world; if order and beauty are reflected in the constitution of the universe, then there is a God."

An 1811 letter to the poet Elsie von der Recke included this: "Heaven rules over the destiny of men and monsters (literally, humans and inhuman beings), and so it will guide me, too, to the better things of life."

A sick friend received the following advice from Beethoven, written in 1816: "It's the same with humanity; here too (in suffering), he must show his strength, i.e., endure without knowing or feeling his nullity, and reach his perfection again for which the Most High wishes to make us worthy."

In an 1810 letter the composer reflected on God: "I haven't a single friend; I must live alone. But well I know that God is nearer to me than to the others of my art; I associate with Him without fear, I have always recognized and understood Him, and I have no fear for my music, it can meet no evil fate. Those who understand it must become free from all the miseries that the others drag with them."

Beethoven showed that he understood that hard work, and

not just self-belief, was necessary for accomplishment when he wrote the following, sometime between 1816 and 1817: "The boundaries are not yet fixed which shall call out to talent and industry: thus far and no further!" This statement, written sometime in the early 1800s, can be interpreted as law of attraction thinking, but also highlights Beethoven's belief in the power of love and beauty: "Hate reacts on those who nourish it."

For Beethoven, the creation of music was the highest spiritual pursuit. That's what he lived for—he used his thoughts and imagination to create music that has resonated throughout the centuries. But none of his compositions would have come to be if he had never put pen to paper and acted upon the notes in his head.

Shakespeare's Company

William Shakespeare was born in April 1564, in Stratford-upon-Avon, although he spent most of his professional life working on the London stage. He was married at eighteen to Anne Hathaway, and the couple had three children. The first was Susanna, followed by fraternal twins Judith and Hamnet, a boy who died sometime during early childhood. Shakespeare had established himself professionally by the early 1590s, not only as a playwright but also as an actor and part owner in an acting company. He earned both critical and commercial success, and, of course, his plays are still performed today on stages from Broadway to small-town high schools. Historians believe Shakespeare retired to Stratford sometime in the early 1600s, probably between 1610 and 1613. He died in 1616.

The best way to interpret what Shakespeare believed about spiritual matters, or religions, at least in the context of *The Secret,* is to look at his texts. Shakespeare wasn't a pagan or a deist—although a lively debate swirls around his religious beliefs. Officially, he was a communicant of the Church of England, and likely believed in the Elizabethan worldview, which was that there was a Great Chain of Being. This concept, which was initiated in classical literature, became essential to both medieval and Renaissance thought. It envisions the universe as a hierarchy established by the Supreme Being, where God stands at the top of a vertical chain. Beneath God are the angels. Beneath the angels is man. Beneath man sit animals, and beneath them are the flora of the earth. Minerals ranked lower than all of the above; however, gold sat at the top of the mineral hierarchy. The place of a being, or thing, on the chain was determined by its ratio of "spirit" to "matter." Man was thought to have the most spirit of all the earthly beings, but of course not having more than angels.

That said, there is currently a lively and vigorous debate going on among Shakespeare experts and aficionados about whether or not the playwright was actually a Roman Catholic. His parents were both Roman Catholics. And if he were sympathetic to or practicing Catholicism, it would have been very dangerous to be open about that fact, given the time in which he lived. Elizabeth I was the sovereign ruler of the country and head of the Church of England during Shakespeare's adulthood. While the court tolerated a range of private religious beliefs, public conformity and loyalty to the state church was expected. Recusancy, meaning the refusal to submit to established authority or the refusal of Roman Catholics to attend services of the Church of England, was punishable by a variety of fines and even imprisonment (or worse).

Another strain of thought suggests that both Catholicism and the Church of England might have turned Shakespeare off.

Stephen Greenblatt's biography of Shakespeare, *Will in the World: How Shakespeare Became Shakespeare* (2004), makes a case for the idea that Shakespeare had a close encounter with religious fanaticism as a young man in Lancashire via a family of recusants who had connections to a Jesuit scholar named Edmund Campion, who was arrested and executed for his missionary activities. Greenblatt argues that the playwright's exposure to missionary zealotry gave way to religious skepticism and a more reasoned sensibility; his plays are often set in England's Catholic past, and frequently blend religion, politics, the occult, and superstition.

In any case, Shakespeare's plays express a variety of points of view, and they do not profess a personal adherence to either the Church of England or Roman Catholicism. Some experts have said that Shakespeare may have had a "hybrid" faith, and held contradictory beliefs. Whatever he believed, the best way to uncover what he may have thought about the cosmic ability for man to attract certain things into his life through thought is best considered by reading what he wrote in his plays. He seems self-directed, interested in the value of education, honesty, and intellectual courage. He, through his character Polonius, wrote the famous and oft-quoted line, "This above all, to thine own self be true."

In addition, many of Shakespeare's tragedies espouse the notion that no matter what we do, we're more or less in the hands of fortune. Many tragedies of the Elizabethan period, including Shakespeare's, followed the convention established by Aristotle, whereby great men suffer from a tragic flaw that dooms them. The flaw is very often hubris. He does say in certain cases that the fault is in men, not the stars, but he has certain characters wonder why good men suffer. The point is, shit happens—and there's nothing we can do about it.

The following quotations may also shed some light on how Shakespeare viewed man's position and power in the universe.

> Cowards die many times before their death; the valiant never taste of death but once.
> —*Julius Caesar,* Act II, Scene 2

> The robb'd that smiles, steals something from the thief.
> —*Othello,* Act I, Scene 3

> Suit the action to the word, the word to the action.
> —*Hamlet,* Act III, Scene 2

> Our doubts are traitors and make us lose the good we oft might win by fearing to attempt.
> —*Measure for Measure,* Act I, Scene 4

> Your If is the only peacemaker; much virtue in If.
> —*As You Like It,* Act V, Scene 4

> But if it be a sin to covet honor, I am the most offending soul alive.
> —*King Henry V,* Act IV, Scene 3

> God has given you one face, and you make yourself another.
> —*Hamlet,* Act III, Scene 1

> There is no darkness but ignorance.
> —*Twelfth Night,* Act IV, Scene 2

And finally, the following, a sentiment not shared by those scores of *Secret* admirers who are busy filling "vision boards" with images of dream homes, cars, designer clothes, and money. This is not to say that one shouldn't create a scrapbook of wants and desires; it's just that Shakespeare may not have approved.

I would not have you to think that my desire of having is the sin of covetousness.

— *Twelfth Night*, Act V, Scene 1

Emerson's Nature of Man

Ralph Waldo Emerson is at the center of the American transcendental movement, setting out most of its ideas and values in *Nature*, which he self-published anonymously in 1836. Emerson's idea of transcendentalism, which was also embraced by Henry David Thoreau, Margaret Fuller, and others, was based on the idea that a perfect spiritual state "transcends" the physical and empirical, and can only be appreciated through an individual's intuition, rather than through religious dogma. There is also a chance that Byrne might have misconstrued Emerson's transcendentalism with the 1960s hippy version, which was much more mystical and magical (and involved acid trips and Mary Quant minidresses) than Emerson would have imagined. Yet it is also true that the New Thought movement felt a kinship with Emerson, whether he liked it or not. The December 1914 issue of the metaphysical periodical *Nautilus* has a full-page ad for an Emerson quotation calendar.

"The secret is the answer to all that there has been, all that is, and all that will ever be." This quote, which Byrne attributes to Emerson, is placed at the end of *The Secret* book. It is an elusive line. My own word search of *Nature, Essays First Series* (which includes "Self-Reliance"), *Essays Second Series, Poems, May Day,* collected letters, *Conduct of Life,* and *Representations* turn up nothing remotely similar. A search of his essays (but not his lectures or journals) turned up nothing either. See for yourself at www.walden.org/Institute/thoreau/about2/E/Emerson_Ralph_Waldo/Concordan/. Of course, my search was of Emerson's most well known, accessible, and popular titles; it could be somewhere more obscure.

Why does it matter whether he said it or not? Because that line and its attribution are now parroted all over the Internet, and in other publications, as a way of validating the Secret (even though it was only given that moniker recently) by virtue of the "fact" that Emerson knew it and believed in the law of attraction. The attribution of quotations is a problem that publishers and scholars have long grappled with. Since I am not an expert on Emerson, it was important to find a specialist who could confirm or deny whether or not Emerson ever said these words.

Harvard professor of American literature Lawrence Buell is the author of, among other titles, *Literary Transcendentalism* (1973), *New England Literary Culture* (1986), and *Emerson* (2003). *Emerson* won the 2003 Warren-Brooks Award for outstanding literary criticism. In a May 2007 e-mail, Buell wrote, "I do believe this is an authentic Emerson quotation, but I can't offhand identify the source."

Others are less sure. Joel Myerson is one such expert. Knowing a bit about his impressive credentials is important in establishing his reliability. He is the Distinguished Professor Emeritus and Distinguished Research Professor in the English Department of the University of South Carolina. He has a Ph.D. from Northwestern University. His areas of expertise include Ralph Waldo Emerson and transcendentalism.

Professor Myerson has written, edited, coauthored, or coedited fifty books, including descriptive primary bibliographies of Emily Dickinson (1984), Emerson (1982, 2005), Fuller (1978), Theodore Parker (1981), and Walt Whitman (1993); collections of Emerson's writings, including *Antislavery Writings* (1995), *Selected Letters* (1997), *Later Lectures* (2001), and *Selected Lectures* (2005), and

Transcendentalism: A Reader (2000); *The Transcendentalists: A Review of Research and Criticism* (1984); collections of essays on Emerson (1982, 1983, 1992, 2000, 2003, 2006) and transcendentalism (1982); and *The Emerson Brothers: A Fraternal Biography in Letters* (2005). He has also published numerous articles in scholarly journals, including *American Literature, American Transcendental Quarterly, Emily Dickinson Journal, Harvard Library Bulletin, Thoreau Journal Quarterly, Thoreau Society Bulletin, Walt Whitman Quarterly Review,* and scores of others.

The professor has delivered papers or chaired sessions at meetings of the American Literature Association, the Association for Documentary Editing, the Australia and New Zealand American Studies Association, the Bibliographical Society of America, the Ralph Waldo Emerson Society, the Thoreau Society, and universities all over the world. He has received grants and fellowships from the American Philosophical Society, the National Endowment for the Humanities, the Guggenheim Foundation, and the South Carolina Committee for the Humanities. Four of his books have been designated by *Choice* as Outstanding Academic Books of the Year. In 2000, he was given the Distinguished Achievement Award of the Ralph Waldo Emerson Society, and in 2004, the Thoreau Society awarded him its highest honor, the Thoreau Society Medal.

There's more I could say about the distinguished career of Professor Myerson, but suffice it to say that the dramatically truncated version of his professional biography noted here demonstrates that he is one of the country's foremost Emerson scholars, a point that cannot be made finely enough. For when I e-mailed him about the Emerson quote early one morning, he replied within the hour with the following response: "I've checked through my concordances to Emerson's works, lectures, and journals, and can't find the quote you sent me. The closest I can find is this: 'We know the answer that leaves nothing to ask,' which is from the essay 'Success' in the 1903–1904 Centenary Edition of Emerson's works published by Houghton, Mifflin, vol. 7, p. 307. As you know from your searches, there are a lot of quotations 'by Emerson' on the Web, without attribution, most of which are not by him."

Okay, so what did Emerson say that can be definitively confirmed and sourced? In the essay "Success" from *Society and Solitude* (1870) he wrote, "Self-trust is the first secret of success, the belief that if you are here the authorities of the universe put you here, and for cause, or with some task strictly appointed you in your constitution, and so long as you work at that you are well and successful."

Emerson's essay "Self-Reliance" could loosely be construed as a form of the law of attraction, in that it requires you to do something for yourself by depending on your "inner man." The following passages, both from "Self-Reliance," give a good indication of Emerson's basic transcendental philosophy.

> Trust thyself: every heart vibrates to that iron string. Accept the place the divine providence has found for you, the society of your contemporaries, the connection of events. Great men have always done so, and confided themselves childlike to the genius of their age, betraying their perception that the absolutely trustworthy was seated at their heart, working through their hands, predominating in all their being. And we are now men, and must accept in the highest mind the same transcendent destiny; and not minors and invalids in a protected corner, not cowards fleeing before a revolution, but guides, redeemers, and benefactors, obeying the Almighty effort, and advancing on Chaos and the Dark.
>
> What I must do is all that concerns me, not what the people think. This rule, equally arduous in actual and in in-

tellectual life, may serve for the whole distinction between greatness and meanness. It is the harder, because you will always find those who think they know what is your duty better than you know it. It is easy in the world to live after the world's opinion; it is easy in solitude to live after our own; but the great man is he who in the midst of the crowd keeps with perfect sweetness the independence of solitude.

Howard P. Segal, Bird Professor of History at the University of Maine, is an expert on America utopianism (which includes the transcendentalists) and is the author of *Technological Utopianism in American Culture* (1985), *Technology in America: A Brief History* (with Alan Marcus, 1989, 1999), and *Recasting the Machine Age: Henry Ford's Village Industries* (2001). Segal says, "Emerson, as you surely know, was no soft-headed romantic but a tough-minded thinker. Optimistic, certainly; but no third-rate 'positive thinker.' He was no Norman Vincent Peale, for example."

A brief look at Emerson's life, which was filled with both personal tragedy and intellectual triumph (he was a popular speaker and public intellectual in his day), indicates just how pragmatic he must have had to become. He was born in 1803, a middle son of four brothers, to a conservative Unitarian minister father and a devout mother. His father died when he was just eight. He also lost all of his brothers, his first wife, Ellen Tucker, and his eldest son, Waldo, when the little fellow was just five.

Emerson studied at Harvard University, but his work there was limited by vision problems. He was ultimately ordained as a minister of the Second Church in Boston in 1829, but resigned when his first wife died, in 1832. He traveled through Europe for a while, and then returned to New England and met and married Lydia Jackson in 1835. They relocated to Concord, Massachusetts, and started a family. Concord became the center of the transcendental movement. Emerson was able to make a comfortable living writing and lecturing. Between 1845 and 1850 he was lecturing widely and frequently on "the uses of great men," which was published in 1850 as *Representative Man*. In 1851, he developed yet another series of lectures, which would be published in 1860 as *The Conduct of Life*.

Ralph Waldo Emerson became the most well-known man of letters in the United States, establishing himself as a prolific poet, essayist, and lecturer and an advocate of social reforms, notably slavery reform. However, he was also skeptical of professional do-gooders. For Emerson, all things exist in a ceaseless flow of change, and "being" is the subject of constant metamorphosis. But this does not mean he believed in the law of attraction or like attracts like. In fact, experts say that his thinking in later years actually shifted from ideas of unity to *the balance of opposites*. Yet, despite some modifications in his philosophy, Emerson always championed the notion of the individual to discover all truth and experience, nonconformity, and the ability to reach the highest degree of consciousness by following our intuition, ideas which influenced other writers, such as Henry David Thoreau and Walt Whitman. Perhaps the idea that Emerson knew the Secret comes from the idea that Emerson believed in self-determination—but that concept is not the same as thinking yourself thin, rich, or famous.

The following passage from "Self-Reliance" best describes Emerson's view of the individual and his ability to act. (Italics are mine.)

> There is a time in every man's education when he arrives at the conviction that envy is ignorance; that imitation is suicide; that he must take himself for better, for worse, as his portion; that though the wide universe is full of good, *no kernel of nourishing corn can come to him but through his toil bestowed on*

that plot of ground which is given to him to till. The power which resides in him is new in nature, and none but he knows what that is which he can do, nor does he know until he has tried. Not for nothing one face, one character, one fact makes much impression on him, and another none. This sculpture in the memory is not without pre-established harmony. The eye was placed where one ray should fall, that it might testify of that particular ray. We but half express ourselves, and are ashamed of that divine idea which each of us represents. It may be safely trusted as proportionate and of good issues, so it be faithfully imparted, but God will not have his work made manifest by cowards. *A man is relieved and gay when he has put his heart into his work and done his best; but what he has said or done otherwise shall give him no peace.* It is a deliverance, which does not deliver. In the attempt his genius deserts him; no muse befriends; no invention, no hope.

Ultimately, it's safe to say that Beethoven, Shakespeare, and Emerson were optimistic men, yet they were also realists who worked very hard at their crafts. All of them, in their own way and within the limits of their eras, were trying to make meaning out of life and humanity. Being philosophical, however, does not necessitate believing specifically that thoughts create reality. It is evident, however, from the prolific body of work of all three men that they understood that thought, when coupled with action and blessed by talent, creates art and beauty.

· 8 ·

Men Who Changed a Century:
Thomas Edison, Winston Churchill,
and Albert Einstein

SEVERAL OF THE twentieth century's most significant figures are mentioned or directly quoted in *The Secret,* with the intention of leading readers to believe they knew about and used the law of attraction. Among them are three men who shifted society through practical invention, public service, and science: Thomas Alva Edison (1847–1931), an American who created the first industrial research lab and developed the phonograph and electric light, among other things; Winston Churchill (1874–1965), the British statesman and prime minister who led the United Kingdom's efforts during World War II; and Albert Einstein (1879–1955), a German-born theoretical physicist famous for developing the theory of relativity and other discoveries in his field.

Books about these three men could fill a library—scholars and historians have made careers out of studying their lives. Instead of encapsulating their lives or reviewing biographical details,

I've tried to use the biographical specifics, as well as their own words, that reveal their beliefs as they relate to the law of attraction. My conclusion, based on research, is that it is doubtful that any one of these three believed in the idea that their thoughts manifested things and events in the metaphysical sense. They were men of their time, men who thought and worked, men with weaknesses and frailties. And sometimes they were wrong. It is up to the curious reader to investigate these men's lives further and see if they agree. There is a wealth of material available; there are several recommended biographies listed in the "Further Reading" section.

No Light at the End of the Tunnel: Thomas Alva Edison

As an inventor Thomas Edison was prolific: He applied for and received 1,093 patents in his lifetime—although his biographers debate how many were the result of his singular genius or those of his assistants who worked in his research lab (a concept he also invented and which is still used today in both universities and industry). He was the first to invent the lightbulb, and he developed what became an electricity distribution system that enabled cities to deliver power simultaneously to multiple homes and businesses.

Edison's famous bullheaded stubbornness and inflexibility resulted in losing businesses and money. He had a tendency to cling to ideas—so convinced was he about their superiority that he was sometimes blinded to opportunity and closed off from other, often better and more commercial, points of view. His negative and positive thinking resulted in fortune and failure. For instance, Edison thought very *negatively* about technological innovations that he saw as threatening to his inventions, and therefore, his business. And his obstinate positivism about some of his ideas did not serve him well all the time, ironically enough. Here, briefly, are two good examples.

First, Edison was *positive* that direct current (DC) was a better way to deliver electricity than alternating current (AC), developed by Nikola Tesla, and used by Edison's rival, George Westinghouse. Maybe Edison proves positive thinking doesn't work, especially since Edison's argument against AC resulted in the development of an efficient electric chair—the peacenik inventor recommended Westinghouse's AC as the cleanest way to kill a man. You can read detailed accounts of his attempt to form an electric company, and the electric chair controversy, in the more than sixty books that have been written about Edison. But briefly, the City of New York favored AC over DC because it was more easily transmitted, it could reach higher voltage, and it could be delivered over thinner and cheaper wires. AC is now the standard in the United States. Ultimately, Edison lost control of the company that continues to bear his name, Consolidated Edison, or ConEd.

Second, Edison developed sound recording, first as a cylinder phonograph and later as disc recordings. He invented and manufactured his own record players, which could only play Edison records (and Edison records could only be played on Edison record players). Other American record companies, Victor and Columbia, made records—called 78s, because they revolved at 78 revolutions per minute—that could be played on each other's machines. Specifically, Edison players used vertical needles, and Victor and Columbia used lateral needles. Edison's records were half an inch thick—much thicker than other companies'. He believed that a record should be able to survive a toss from a second-story window. I have personally witnessed a test of this and it proves to be true: Edison records *are* virtually indestructible.

However, you may not want to listen to what's on them. That's because the other problem with Edison records was their limited subject matter. Edison only recorded music that reflected his taste, which was popular but narrow, and he lost a lot of market share because of this. A classic example: He recorded very little jazz and very few African American groups. Other companies noticed a market for African American music, not only within the black community, but also among whites. Edison's company recorded a tiny handful of black artists. No amount of positive thinking on Edison's part could make people buy music they didn't want to listen to.

The final irony in terms of his recording company was Edison's resistance to electric recording with microphones—which was a direct extension of an electronic principle he had developed! In 1925 and 1926 all the other leading companies of the day went into electrical recording. Edison refused. By the time he admitted defeat, in 1928, and went into electrical recording, it was too late because of the Depression. Edison was very shortly out of the recording and manufacturing business entirely. Clearly, Edison believing something to be true did not make it a reality.

Edison did have religious and spiritual beliefs that bordered on the metaphysical, but I'm not convinced that this is proof he believed in the law of attraction. He also dabbled in the occult, and in 1920 he tried to invent a contraption that could communicate with the dead—it didn't work. It is believed to have been a telephone with a really loud receiver. Edison was duped by a magician, Berthold "Bert" Reese, whom he met through his friend Henry Ford (see Chapter 9 for more on Ford). Reese's tricks included fake displays of extrasensory perception, or ESP. Edison's insistence that Reese was the real deal—a genuine mind reader—led *New York Times* journalist Edward Marshall to write an extensive article on Sunday, November 13, 1910, and a follow-up article with illustrations a week later, explaining how Reese might have done his tricks. Reese was ultimately shown to be a trickster and an entertainer, despite Edison's protests to the contrary.

As far as other religious beliefs, Edison wavered between atheism and belief in God. In 1911, this is what Edison told Edward Marshall, now writing for *The Columbian* magazine.

> I never have denied Supreme Intelligence. What I have denied and what my reason compels me to deny, is the existence of a Being throned above us as a god, directing our mundane affairs in detail, regarding us as individuals, punishing us, rewarding us as human judges might. I do not wish to have the public think that I deny the merit of the world's great moral teachers—Confucius, Buddha, Christ. They were great men—truly wonderful. Their teachings are summed up in the Golden Rule, and any man who follows that will be far higher and far happier than any man who does not. But the worship of an individual God is not a necessary detail of following the Golden Rule.
>
> A man is not an individual; he is a vast collection of a myriad of individuals, just as a city is. The cell, minute and little known, is the real and only individual. A man is made of many million cells. His intelligence consists of the combined intelligence of them all, as a city's is made up of the combined intelligence of its inhabitants. Not being, in effect, an individual, how could he go to heaven or hell as an individual, be given a reward or any punishment, after death had caused the separation of his cells and the diffusion of their collective intelligence?

Edison might have indulged his curiosity for the paranormal, but he spent more time directing his Menlo Park, New Jersey, research assistants and figuring out ways to make money from his patents than he did thinking positive thoughts about them. He was a big believer in hard work as a way to achieve success. According to biographer Neil Baldwin (*Edison: Inventing the Century*, 1995), Edison attributed all his accomplishments to hard work. Baldwin describes how Edison would receive letters from scores of people, requesting the secret of his success. To one, Edison replied, "I work 18 hours daily—have been doing this for 45 years. This is double the usual amount men do. . . . The reason I can work 18 hours is because I eat very little, sleep very little, and wear clothes that do not pinch the blood veins in the slightest."

Edison is also famous for this *bon mot:* "Genius is one percent inspiration and ninety-nine percent perspiration," quoted in an interview with him published in a 1932 edition of *Harper's Monthly*. Several other verifiable quotes, carefully researched by George S. Bryan in *Edison: The Man and His Work* (1926), reflect Edison's take on his success and creativity. Some border on the metaphysical: for example, these quotes, from an interview by W. P. Warren, "Edison on Inventors and Inventions," published in *Century Magazine* in July 1911: "Imagination supplies the ideas, and technical knowledge carries them out." "I always keep within a few feet of the earth's surface all the time. At least I never let my thoughts run up higher than the Himalayas." "Science cannot reach any other conclusion than that there is a great intelligence manifested everywhere."

Despite Edison's on-and-off penchant for the magical and the mysterious, and his shifting views about God and the afterlife, his own life work, which was to invent items that would make him money by virtue of their general usefulness, provides the clearest insight into the man. His ability to worker harder and longer than most people gave him a leg up on the competition.

Statesman, Skeptic: Winston Churchill

Winston Churchill was a complex man whose life has been chronicled in detail, by both Churchill himself and numerous biographers. He was the son of Randolph Churchill, a Conservative politician, and Jennie Jerome, the daughter of New York businessman Leonard Jerome. He went to the Royal Military College and was a member of the British Army, fighting in India and the Sudan. While in the military, he acted as a war correspondent for *The Daily Telegraph.* He left the army in 1899 and became a correspondent for *The Morning Post.* While reporting on the Boer War he was kidnapped and made headlines in England when he escaped. In 1900, he wrote a book about the experience, called *London to Ladysmith.* Indeed, Churchill was a prolific author and wrote numerous books on English and world history for which he won the Nobel Prize for Literature in 1953.

Churchill entered politics in 1900 and continued to serve in a variety of capacities and in different parties, changing his affiliation from right to left to right again for many years—details of which can be found in any number of biographies. He also published more books. After Adolf Hitler gained power in Germany in 1933, Churchill advocated rearmament and opposed the Conservative government's appeasement policy. In 1939, Churchill's argument that Britain and France should form a military alliance with the Soviet Union was met with a great deal of homegrown controversy.

I am cutting the story short, but Neville Chamberlain decided to resign as prime minister amidst criticism of his policies, and on May 10, 1940, King George VI appointed Churchill as prime minister. On the same day the German army began its western offensive, and two days later it occupied France. Historians say

Churchill's ability to rally the British people through his carefully constructed speeches helped lead the country's march to victory. He loved to drink, especially whiskey, and was given to bouts of depression—not a characteristic you associate with a positive thinker.

The Secret's Web site says that Churchill is a law of attraction "teacher" because he believed in never giving up, and quotes him as saying that "the empires of the future are the empires of the mind." But we should not confuse Churchill's belief in the power of intelligence and reason with positive thinking. Given Churchill's rather pragmatic intellectual life, it seems really odd that he would have said, "You create your own universe as you go along," a quote that appears in both book and the DVD. Did Churchill really believe that? Well, it turns out he did write that line; it is from one of his autobiographical books, *My Early Life: 1874–1904,* originally published in 1930, reissued in 1958 by Charles Scribner's Sons, and reissued a second time in 1996 by Touchstone, an imprint of Simon & Schuster, which publishes *The Secret.* The context of the quote (found on page 117 of the Touchstone edition) explains a lot; clearly it was misused in Byrne's book.

> The idea that nothing is true except what we comprehend is silly, and that ideas which our minds cannot reconcile are mutually destructive, sillier still. Certainly nothing could be more repulsive both to our minds and feelings than the spectacle of thousands of millions of universes—for that is what they say it comes to now—all knocking about together for ever without any rational or good purpose behind them. I therefore adopted quite early in life a system of believing whatever I wanted to believe, while at the same time leaving reason to pursue unfettered whatever paths she was capable of treading.

> Some of my cousins who had the great advantage of University education used to tease me with arguments to prove that nothing has any existence except what we think of it. The whole creation is but a dream; all phenomena are imaginary. You create your own universe as you go along. The stronger your imagination, the more variegated your universe. When you leave off dreaming, the universe ceases to exist. These amusing mental acrobatics are all right to play with. They are perfectly harmless and perfectly useless. I warn my younger readers only to treat them as a game. The metaphysicians will have the last word and defy you to disprove their absurd propositions.

In *Winston Churchill* (2002), author John Keegan helps to further set the record straight on Churchill's spiritual beliefs. He says that Churchill had a profound moral sense and deep spiritual feelings, but neither had a metaphysical basis. Keegan believes that if Churchill had been pressed to name the source of his spirituality, he might have said it came from "historical universals" from the humanist tradition, religious grounding that was conventional and inherited from his family, and influences of piety and goodness from his "beloved nanny, Mrs. Everest; in the code of schoolboy fair play; and in the ethic of manliness learned at the Royal Military College."

Albert Einstein: Not Very Attractive

Rhonda Byrne writes that Einstein knew "a great deal of *The Secret*" (apparently he wasn't smart enough to know all of it). Einstein is a figure who has achieved cult status in both the scientific world and popular culture. A massive new biography has recently hit the shelves—Walter Isaacson's *Einstein: His Life and Universe*—and another classic life story has been reissued—the late Ronald Clark's 1971 *Einstein: The Life and Times*—adding to the already impressive list of books and articles that have been written about the theoretical physicist and mathematician. Everyone from rock stars to auto mechanics to TV producers have embraced Einstein's ideas, leaving open the door to possible misinterpretation. That's why I am treading lightly here and will only attempt to answer one question: Did Einstein believe that our thoughts are sent out to the universe and result in the manifestation of events or things? I draw this conclusion from Einstein's own words, as written by him or as reported on by credible authorities. It seems fairly certain that Einstein did not believe in the law of attraction.

Some experts say that Einstein believed free will was an illusion and *we are at the mercy of the universal laws.* If we accept that this is true, then we have to agree that Einstein probably also believed that trying to control reality through *the free will of our directed thoughts* is a useless and futile exercise—in other words, the universe has a plan and our thoughts are immaterial to it. Walter Isaacson's recent biography of Einstein was excerpted in the April 5, 2007, issue of *Time* magazine. In it, Isaacson says Einstein wrote the following: "Schopenhauer's saying, 'A man can do as he wills, *but not will as he wills,*' has been a real inspiration to me since my youth; it has been a continual consolation in the face of life's hardships, my own and others', and an unfailing wellspring of tolerance."

Albert Einstein: The Human Side (1979), edited by Banesh Hoffman and Helen Dukas, indicates that the scientist likely did not worship at the temple of the law of attraction.

I cannot conceive of a personal God who would directly influence the actions of individuals, or would directly sit in judgment on creatures of his own creation. I cannot do this in spite of the fact that mechanistic causality has, to a certain extent, been placed in doubt by modern science. My religiosity consists in a humble admiration of the infinitely superior spirit that reveals itself in the little that we, with our weak and transitory understanding, can comprehend of reality. Morality is of the highest importance—but for us, not for God.

The mystical trend of our time, which shows itself particularly in the rampant growth of the so-called Theosophy and Spiritualism, is for me no more than a symptom of weakness and confusion. Since our inner experiences consist of reproductions, and combinations of sensory impressions, the concept of a soul without a body seems to me to be empty and devoid of meaning.

In "Science, Philosophy, and Religion, A Symposium," published by the Conference on Science, Philosophy and Religion in Their Relation to the Democratic Way of Life, New York, 1941, Einstein made this point about religion.

To be sure, the doctrine of a personal God interfering with the natural events could never be refuted, in the real sense, by science, for this doctrine can always take refuge in those domains in which scientific knowledge has not yet been able to set foot. But I am persuaded that such behavior on the part of the representatives of religion would not only be unworthy but also fatal. For a doctrine which is able to maintain itself not in clear light but only in the dark, will of necessity lose its effect on mankind, with incalculable harm to human progress. . . . If it is one of the goals of religions to liberate mankind as far as possible from the bondage of egocentric cravings, desires, and fears, scientific reasoning can aid religion in another sense.

Einstein's view of metaphysics was not particularly generous, according to the late biographer Ronald W. Clark. In *Einstein:*

The Life and Times he writes, "Einstein was now among the 'European professors distinguished in philosophy and science' and as such he supported in the summer of 1912 the foundation of a scientific association 'quite indifferent to metaphysical speculation and so-called metaphysical and transcendental doctrines' and 'opposed to all metaphysical undertakings.'" Clark says that this underlines Einstein's conviction that special relativity was not the result of metaphysical speculation, but of scientific experimental evidence.

The Secret states that Einstein said "thank you" to all the scientists who came before him "hundreds of times each day." According to Clifford M. Will, the James S. McDonnell professor of physics at Washington University in St. Louis, Missouri, Einstein may have *said* that he did so, as a way of acknowledging the important contributions of predecessors. "But we don't say thank-you a hundred times a day, or even once a day, and again, I can't imagine Einstein doing this literally," Will wrote in an April 2007 e-mail. "[Isaac] Newton (who has been the subject of wacko theories à la *Da Vinci Code* and others) was famously quoted as saying that, if he had seen further than others it was because he had stood on the shoulders of giants. You might think he was thanking his predecessors in the spirit of *The Secret,* but in fact he was also insulting his rival, Robert Hooke, who happened to be a hunchback," Will explains. "So you have to be careful when you make something out of what people say."

Dennis Overbye, science writer for *The New York Times* and author of *Einstein in Love* (2001), says it is doubtful that Einstein would believe in the law of attraction. "He thought that the idea of a personal god who pays attention to what we are up to is a childish notion," he says. "Einstein used the word 'god' a lot, so people mistake it for a spiritual or conventional notion, but he used it as shorthand for the rationality and mystery of nature—the mystery of why is it here at all and why is it understandable," he explains. Einstein experienced the universe as magical, according to Overbye, and it is fair to regard it as a deep puzzle. "Comprehension of that mystery was one of the most profound experiences for Einstein, but it was not one that he thought would reach out and help you get past your exam next week."

Finally, the following telling (and verifiable) passage may finally put to rest the question of Einstein's belief in the metaphysics of "ask, believe, receive." It comes from a response Einstein gave to a child who had written to him in 1936 asking if scientists pray, and published in *Albert Einstein: The Human Side:* "Scientific research is based on the idea that everything that takes place is determined by laws of nature, and therefore this holds for the action of people. For this reason, a research scientist will hardly be inclined to believe that events could be influenced by a prayer, i.e., by a wish addressed to a Supernatural Being."

Case closed.

The Challenge of Accuracy

Research into *The Secret*'s characterization of the figures in this chapter and others in this section has raised troubling concerns over the authenticity and context of quotes that have been attributed to them, not just in *The Secret,* but in other metaphysical books and on the Internet.

Long before the advent of the Web, which has made the dissemination of information, both real and imagined, run at lightening speed, Thomas Edison expressed his annoyance at having quotes attributed to him that he never said. In the January 12, 1901, issue of *Electrical Review,* the inventor and businessman complained, "The worst of it is that these fellows who come out here [to West Orange, New Jersey] go back without having seen me or heard me speak a word and write out alleged interviews that make me seem foolish to those who don't know me."

Einstein was also irritated over being misquoted. In a February 22, 1949, letter to journalist Max Brod, quoted in *The Human Side,* the scientist laments: "There have already been published by the bucketful such brazen lies and utter fictions about me that I would have long since gone to my grave if I had let myself pay attention to them." He might be amused to see this quote attributed to him in *The Secret:* "Imagination is everything. It is the preview of life's coming attractions." Alice Calaprice, a former in-house editor at Princeton University Press and author of the book *The New Quotable Einstein,* says no dice. She should know. Einstein's writings and presumed remarks are vast—forty-five thousand documents alone are housed in his archive in Jerusalem—and Calaprice is the only person who has taken the trouble to chase down the provenance of many of Einstein's reported remarks, with much work and scholarship.

"They're made up," she says with a laugh, regarding the sentences in question, "It's easy to write something and put his name under it." Calaprice cites an authentic, verifiable Einsteinism about imagination from an interview conducted by George Sylvester Viereck entitled, "What Life Means to Einstein," published in the October 26, 1929, issue of *The Saturday Evening Post:* "Imagination is more important than knowledge. Knowledge is limited. Imagination encircles the world."

This begs the question, what would Einstein and Churchill, or Emerson for that matter, have thought about being lumped in with modern-day metaphysicians via quotes that they may or may not have originated, or words taken out of context in a way that they did not intend? The two quotes attributed to Churchill and Emerson discussed here are now being parroted all over the Internet, in connection with the men's supposed belief in the law of attraction. How sad if people take this misinformation at face value, without looking deeper. If *The Secret* is true, why use bogus information to back it up?

· 9 ·

The Secret Business of Money:
Andrew Carnegie,
William Clement Stone,
and Henry Ford

MUCH OF *The Secret* is directed at the acquisition of wealth, so it follows that a few captains of industry would be mentioned or quoted in it. Promotional trailers for the DVD dramatize old-time business tycoons hiding the Secret from their employees and the public in an effort to keep the information all to themselves, for their own gain. Yet, the three business titans who jump out from Byrne's text—Andrew Carnegie, William Clement Stone, and Henry Ford—didn't keep their success strategies closeted in the least.

Stone, in fact, wrote books about what he called PMA, or positive mental attitude. Carnegie was the alleged inspiration of one of the bestselling books of all time on the topic *Think and Grow Rich* by Napoleon Hill. According to *The Secret*'s Web site, Carnegie taught the Secret to many of history's "greats." So obviously, he wasn't suppressing anything. Ford wasn't a secretive man by nature, and there's little indication that he attributed his success to mental science.

Like so many other boldface names in *The Secret,* Carnegie and Stone are mentioned only in passing. However, both are significant to the themes in *The Secret.* Byrne spends a bit more time on Ford. Since all of them made their own money and since, according to Byrne, you are using *The Secret* (whether or not you know it or believe in it) if you make money, it's worth looking at these men to see what they believed, and how exactly they made their fortunes—through positive thought or positive action or both.

Andrew Carnegie: Rags to Riches

Andrew Carnegie had a lifelong interest in scientific research and in 1902 he set up the Carnegie Institution in Washington. Its mission, following Carnegie's wishes, is to be a home for exceptional individual scientists. Contrary to what Byrne states in *The Secret,* however, it's doubtful that Carnegie saw his own work as a businessman in terms of quantum mechanics.

Carnegie was born in 1835 in Dunfermline, Scotland, to a working-class family. His father, Will, was a skilled weaver who lost his job when, in 1847, steam-powered looms replaced the need for manual labor. Like so many displaced Scottish, Irish, and English workers of the day, the Carnegie family emigrated to the United States, where they settled in Pittsburgh. According to an August 12, 1919, feature story in *The New York Times,* one day after Will Carnegie's death, the young Andrew got his first job, as a bobbin boy in a textile mill. He was thirteen years old. Later he tended a steam engine in another factory and also worked as a messenger boy and a telegraph operator. His role as personal telegrapher and assistant to Thomas Scott, the superintendent of the Pennsylvania Railroad's western division, changed Carnegie's life. There he learned the ins and outs of the train business and made important business connections that would serve him well later in his career. An incredible work ethic was only part of Carnegie's success story—shrewd investments and a talent at managing money enabled him to build his fortune and make lucrative acquisitions. For example, in 1856, he took out a bank loan of a little more than $200 to buy into the Woodruff Sleeping Car Company. Just two years later, he was making about $5,000 annually from the firm. Meanwhile, he continued to work for the Pennsylvania Railroad and was eventually named superintendent of its western division. He took the money he made from the Woodruff Sleeping Car Company and put it into an oil company in Titusville, Pennsylvania. He also invested in the Piper and Schiffler Company, the Adams Express Company, and the Central Transportation Company.

In 1865, Carnegie retired from the railroad, and started devoting himself full-throttle to entrepreneurship. He founded the Keystone Bridge Company, and two years later he formed the Keystone Telegraph Company. In 1868, in what could be considered a Secret-style visualization, Carnegie wrote himself a letter (or affirmation, if you will), outlining his plans for the future. These included resigning from business at age thirty-five, living on an annual income of $50,000, and giving the rest of his money to philanthropic causes. But in 1872, he put off that plan during a visit to a steel plant in England. Realizing the potential of steel in the United States, Carnegie made up his mind to invest in the industry at home; in 1875 he opened the Edgar Thomson Works, in Braddock, Pennsylvania. The company's first order, not surprisingly, was for 2,000 steel rails for the Pennsylvania Railroad.

Carnegie continued to build and acquire manufacturing plants. He also started to write. In 1886, he published an essay in *Forum Magazine* defending the right of workers to unionize, and his book, *Triumphant Democracy,* a celebration of capitalism, became a bestseller. In 1887, Carnegie had a disagreement with one of his business partners, Henry Clay Frick, about a striking union in one of their companies. Carnegie forced Frick to settle with the workers, and thereafter became known as a friend to the working stiff. That view would change later on, in 1892, when he directed Frick to handle another factory strike by hiring Pinkerton agents (a private detective agency used to quell strikers, among other things) to shoot it out with workers, a gun battle that lasted nearly twelve hours. The Pinkertons gave up, the state militia was sent in to reclaim the mill, and strikebreakers were hired to reopen it. That episode ended Carnegie's reputation as a defender of the little guy.

In between strikes and business as usual, Carnegie penned *Gospel of Wealth* (1889), which argued that the wealthy had a moral obligation to give away the money they made to social and educational causes. A few years later, in 1901, Carnegie sold his steel interests to J. P. Morgan for $480 million, and in doing so became the world's richest man. He spent the rest of his years doing good works, as he predicted he would several years before. In 1902, he founded the Carnegie Institution to provide research for American colleges and universities. Later he established the Carnegie Endowment for International Peace (1910) and the Carnegie Corporation (1911), which provided aid to colleges, universities, technical schools, and scientific research. He ended up using much of his fortune to establish or fund many philanthropic and educational institutions.

Carnegie did give some thought to how he was able go from uneducated bobbin boy to multimillionaire while many of his contemporaries still toiled in factories, or worse. David Nasaw, who is the Arthur M. Schlesinger, Jr., professor of American history at the City University of New York and author of *Andrew Carnegie* (2006), the industrialist was not a man of faith and did not believe that a supreme being was responsible for his divine wealth. Nor did Carnegie think his success was due to hard work, especially since he had gotten to the point where he needed to spend only a few hours a day managing his businesses. Carnegie outlined his conclusion in a 1906 essay, "Gospel of Wealth II," published in the *North American Review:* that an individual's wealth was a product of his community. "The railroad stock of the first millionaire would have remained worthless had the communities his railroads served not soared in population," writes Nasaw.

In 1908, Napoleon Hill, a young freelance journalist who was working his way through college, claimed to have interviewed Carnegie. According to Hill, the famous magnate told him "the secret" to his great success. The meeting is not chronicled in any Carnegie biographies I reviewed, and Hill's name goes unmentioned. Professor Nasaw says it's not clear whether the interview ever took place. "I really do not know. The name [Napoleon Hill] never came up in the thousands of pages of letters I read to and from Carnegie, or in the thousands of other documents I reviewed." However, Carnegie was known to greet visitors in his later years, Nasaw continues, so it's possible the two men met and Carnegie never recorded the occasion. "Lots of people came to see him. He was a friendly, likable character." It is even less certain that Carnegie imparted a law of attraction "secret" to Hill, because, according to Nasaw, that was not in line with the magnate's business philosophy. "What he did believe in, his motto, was 'All grows better.' That came from the British philosopher Herbert Spencer [who applied the theory of evolution to philosophy]," and is very different from the law of attraction, like attracts like, or thoughts create things.

Carnegie saw the world in terms of evolutionary laws, again an idea taken from Spencer, meaning that every generation will be more prosperous than the last. They will have more money, more peace, and less poverty. "One can say that is positive thinking, but

Carnegie would not have used that term," says Nasaw. "Carnegie had no real business philosophy other than the one Charles Schwab talked about, which is watch the costs and the profits will take care of themselves. If you keep your costs down you will be able to make money in good times and bad. He understood that nothing stays still and everything is changing, and if you want to be a good businessman you have to look ahead—what is primary today may not be primary tomorrow." As far as the rest of it, Nasaw asserts that Carnegie believed he was lucky that he landed in Pittsburgh at a time when the city was destined to be the manufacturing center of iron and steel and had a locational advantage as the east-west terminus for trains.

Unquestionably, Andrew Carnegie did influence Hill. If the interview actually did take place, Hill may have ascribed certain meanings to the conversation that Carnegie himself did not intend, as when a starstruck kid meets a favorite celebrity and thinks a meaningful personal connection has been made. Hill maintained that Carnegie challenged the young writer to seek out five hundred wealthy people and figure out if there was a similar pattern to how they made their money. So, just like Byrne, he sought out experts who were alive at the time, to learn more about how they made their millions. The result was two books by Hill, both published long after Carnegie died in 1919. The first, *The Law of Success,* was published in 1928, and the second, *Think and Grow Rich,* published in 1937, became a bestseller.

What is interesting about *Think and Grow Rich* is the language it uses to explain a thirteen-part formula for success—it refers to "the secret" and "Carnegie's secret." What is this secret, according to Hill? A positive attitude and the law of attraction! References to *Think and Grow Rich* are oddly absent from either the book or the DVD versions of *The Secret,* although it is mentioned in passing on the Andrew Carnegie page of the Web site. *Think and Grow Rich* has never been out of print since it was first published; it has sat on a variety of business and general bestseller lists during its lifetime and it has never been banned, buried, hidden from view, or kept from the public.

Trailers for the DVD of *The Secret* claim that unnamed businessmen paid vast amounts of money for the Secret and agreed that it would never be released to the public—in fact, the Secret was banned in 1933, say these trailers, but they never explain by whom or why. I can find no evidence of any New Thought books or *Think and Grow Rich* having been banned, although there is an unverifiable story that the Catholic Church banned Haanel's *The Master Key System* in 1933. By parsing out his mysterious-sounding information in weekly installments, Haanel made the information seem proprietary, a clever marketing play. Haanel also charged a princely sum for his information, but it was certainly not the only source of law of attraction literature. Any one of the businessmen who paid for the series could have just as easily picked up a copy of Wallace Wattles's *The Science of Getting Rich,* or bought a copy of *Nautilus,* and for much less money.

At any rate, here's what Hill writes in *Think and Grow Rich:* "Truly, thoughts are things," "All achievement, all earned riches, have their beginning in an idea," "When you begin to THINK AND GROW RICH, you will observe that riches begin with a state of mind—with definiteness of purpose and with little or no hard work," and, "Success comes to those who become SUCCESS-CONSCIOUS. Failure comes to those who indifferently allow themselves to become FAILURE-CONSCIOUS." (The capital letters are Hill's conceit, one that he employs frequently throughout the book.). Hill is all about taking action—no dreamy-eyed couch potatoes allowed! He was big on conferences and Master Mind groups, which he said could be used for problem solving. Anyone who has ever gone to a corporate brainstorming session can thank Napoleon Hill for the privilege. It is clear that Hill's book inspired much of the prosperity literature that has come after *Think and Grow Rich*. Finally, Hill's most famous aphorism has a real "ask, believe, receive" ring to it: "Whatever the mind of man can conceive and believe, the mind of man can achieve, through a positive mental attitude."

Charles Haanel's 1912 *The Master Key System* may have influenced Hill more than his meeting with Andrew Carnegie. Lore has it that the journalist wrote a fan letter to Haanel around 1920 praising the author's work and the influence it had on him. It's not impossible—and Hill certainly could have been exposed to New Thought literature. *Think and Grow Rich* is not that different in essence from *The Master Key System,* or Wallace Wattles's *The Science of Getting Rich,* or any of the other books of that earlier era. However, Hill writes better and is more fun and easier to read than Wattles, who, despite his brevity (*Getting Rich* is a little more than pamphlet length), is turgid and fussy. *Think and Grow Rich* isn't couched in New Thought metaphysical-speak, possibly making it more palatable to people who didn't want their moneymaking advice mixed up with the occult or religion (the words "God," "supreme being," and "Bible" are not found in the book's index). *Think and Grow Rich* had timing on its side too—it was published at the end of Depression, when the economy had started to improve but before the United States entered World War II, so people were once again hopeful. The book was met with a bigger and more eager audience than even the most popular New Thought publications had been in their day.

The Napoleon Hill Foundation continues to spread the gospel of *Think and Grow Rich*. The man himself lived a long life; he died in 1970 at age eighty-seven, having spent much of his life promoting his wealth-and-success philosophy. But it wasn't all roses for Napoleon. Before he wrote his bestseller, he lost his shirt and his house (along with his plans to open the world's first success university) in the stock market crash of 1929. Hill wrote articles for *Inspiration Magazine* and sold a "mental dynamite" program over the next several years. He wrote and sold *The Napoleon Hill Magazine,* advertising it regularly, including in *The New York Times.* On December 4, 1921, a small display ad promised "success in any undertaking" for the price of a subscription.

In a front-page story on May 18, 1930, *The New York Times* reported that Hill was on the receiving end of a restraining order, along with Lester Park and the Corianton Corporation. The men were selling stock in a company organized to promote a motion picture about love and murder among the early American settlers. Hill promoted investment in the film's company, Corianton, to his students and clients in a letter that extolled Park's experience as a film producer. The deputy attorney general, Abraham Davis, maintained that the stock should not be sold to the public because Park had never produced a successful movie, the film was not in production, and the stock was owned personally by Mr. Park, not the Corianton Corporation.

Despite these minor setbacks, Hill eventually wrote and published *Think and Grow Rich* in 1937 and started making money again. Around the time of writing his magnum opus he divorced his wife, Florence, and married a younger, prettier version, Rosa Lee Beeland. She wrote her own book, *How to Attract Men and Money,* evidently from firsthand experience, since she shortly left Hill, taking much of his money with her in a divorce settlement.

Hill eventually remarried and spent the rest of his days marketing his success literature; in the process, he earned the backing of yet another wealthy businessman, William Clement Stone. In fact, so enamored was Stone of Hill that he served as chairman of the board of the Napoleon Hill Foundation for over forty years. Hill is the only person known to have documented his meeting with Carnegie, so we only have his account to go by. Hill was certainly shrewd to wait until Carnegie was long gone before he used his name in conjunction with his own work, making it that much more difficult to call his claim into question. Does it really matter? Perhaps it's enough that Hill was inspired by the life and accomplishments of Andrew Carnegie—a testament to the lasting impact this real-life Horatio Alger has had on American ambitions and aspirations.

Thinking Man's Disciple: William Clement Stone

In the beginning of *The Secret*'s chapter on money, W. Clement Stone is quoted as saying: "Whatever the mind . . . can conceive it can achieve." This is followed by a story by *Chicken Soup for the Soul* mogul Jack Canfield about his own life-changing encounter with the millionaire. There is no doubt that Stone was a believer in the law of attraction. In addition to being an astute businessman (he made his money through insurance companies), he was a success guru who believed in and promoted positive mental attitude, or PMA. In fact, he made a second career as a motivational speaker and writer, coauthoring a book with Napoleon Hill called *Success Through a Positive Mental Attitude*. Stone also developed a series of lectures with Hill called "PMA: Science of Success" and wrote *The Success System That Never Fails* (1962), as well as *The Other Side of the Mind* (1964), which he coauthored with Norma Lee Browning.

Stone was a tough old bird. Born in Chicago on May 4, 1902, he lived to be one hundred, his life spanning an entire century (he passed away on September 3, 2002). With a persona straight from central casting, he was a diminutive man who sported a pencil-thin mustache, and had a penchant for bow ties. He told *Washington Post* reporter Sarah Booth Conroy that his collection numbered 250—he believed bow-tie wearers to be "full of vim and vigor, aggressive and full of drive. They are the best salesmen and entrepreneurs." (Now there's a secret!). The January 26, 1986, article was in part a response to a dress-for-success column in *Success Magazine* by John T. Molloy, who said people don't trust bow-tie wearers. Ironically, Stone founded *Success*, but did not fire Molloy after the article appeared. The insurance tycoon was known for his fashion sense beyond neckwear—he favored hand-tailored suits, patterned vests, bright suspenders, and alligator shoes, and he wore a gold watch with diamond numerals.

Stone may have been short, but his personality was tall. Whenever he felt a companion's attention flag, he'd shout "Bingo!" to bring them back. Every day started with the following mantra: "I feel happy! I feel healthy! I feel terrific!" In fact, Stone talked in exclamation points a good deal of the time. "No battle of any importance can be won without enthusiasm," he told Forrest Wallace Cato in his last interview, which was subsequently published in *The Register* in August 2006.

Stone's education in the school of hard knocks was crucial in forming his philosophy. His was just three when his father died, leaving the family impoverished by gambling losses. At age six, Stone went to work selling newspapers on Chicago's South Side, and by the time he was thirteen, he owned his own newsstand. A November 10, 1963, story in *The New York Times* chronicles what happened next—he stayed with a family in Chicago, continuing to work at odd jobs after his mother had pawned her jewelry and traveled to Detroit to buy a small insurance agency. He eventually followed her there and helped make cold calls, which he called "gold calls."

At age twenty-one, with $100 in his pocket, he established his own insurance agency in 1922, called the Combined Registry Company, according to the *Times*. In just eight years, he had created a sales force of a thousand "poorly trained agents," which he sought to rectify by traveling across the country and training a new team of three hundred, who ended up writing more business than the original, larger army of men. In 1939, he transferred the registry business to Combined Mutual, and in 1947 he merged it into the Combined Insurance Company of America, a stock company. His combined company eventually merged into the Ryan Insurance Group in 1982 and changed its name to the Aon Corporation in 1987. In the book he wrote with Napoleon Hill, he describes his favorite way to acquire businesses, using OPM, which stands for Other People's Money. He urged his readers to do the same: "If you don't have money, use OPM!" He also used PMA, of course.

Like Hill, Stone was pragmatic about PMA and the law of attraction and its usefulness in making money. He didn't muck it up with quantum mechanics, although he did link success to God's divine hand and his own can-do initiative. "Master the art of tapping into the power of your subconscious through your conscious mind regarding emotions, instincts, feelings, tendencies, moods, the formation of desirable habits, and the neutralizing, or elimination of the undesirable," he told Forrest Wallace Cato. What differentiates Stone's view of mind power from that of *The Secret*'s is his insistence that in order for a thought to be manifested in reality, it had to be followed by action. You can't just sit around and think good thoughts. You've got to do something about them. "Regular investment in study, thinking, and planning time, plus following through with action work! Given the necessary experience of doing the right thing the right way, you get the right results consistently. And when you do, work becomes fun," he explained to Cato.

Stone gave away some of his fortune (although not as large a percentage as steel magnate Andrew Carnegie) to many charities and philanthropic causes. On October 28, 1970, *Times* reporter Barbara Campbell followed Stone to visit a drug rehabilitation center he had financed in the Bronx. The excursion included a visit to a "shooting gallery" and a tenement building where a family whom the center was helping lived. There he met seventeen-year-old Angel Sanchez, the one son in the family who had not tried drugs and who had a part-time job in the post office. Angel hoped to finish high school and go the collage, which pleased Stone, who said he would send the young man some books on positive thinking when he returned to Chicago.

Stone also became a high-profile figure in a campaign donation inquiry—he financed millions of dollars of gifts to the campaigns of Richard M. Nixon. His contributions of more than $2 million to Nixon's 1972 reelection campaign, and to the former president's previous campaigns and Republican campaigns in general, were cited in congressional debates after Watergate as a reason for instituting campaign-spending limits. He was also the subject of an IRS inquiry in 1974 over federal gift taxes. Stone said he admired Nixon for his determination and overcoming his defeats for the presidency in 1960 and the California governorship in 1962. Ever the positive thinker, even Watergate couldn't diminish Stone's belief in PMA. He called the scandal a good thing, in that it empowered attorneys general to bring charges against wayward public officials, whereas before Nixon's day wrongdoing was simply swept under the rug.

Henry Ford and the Wheels of Fortune

Byrne writes that Henry Ford knew both the Secret *and* the law of the universe—and, according to *The Secret*'s Web site, he learned them from Andrew Carnegie. This is quite ironic, since, according to Ford authorities, the man was barely literate, highly provincial, naïvely uninterested in the modern world, and to top it all off, a raging anti-Semite who was adored by Hitler. With the help of professional writers, Ford composed a series of notorious essays about the "Jewish problem," now published in book form, and continues to be a favorite today among both the extreme right and the radical left, feeding both groups' tendency to blame the ills of the world on Jews and/or Israel.

Henry Ford was born on July 30, 1863, the first of six children of William and Mary Ford, in what is now Dearborn, Michigan. The family ran a prosperous farm, and Henry enjoyed a typical rural nineteenth-century childhood, rising early to help with household tasks and attending a one-room schoolhouse with his siblings. However, he did not particularly like life on the farm and the chores that went with it. He was much more interested in, and very good at, mechanical work. "Ford was a farm boy who hated farming but wanted all of his workers to be part-time farmers. He was rooted in rural America despite his own contributions to increasing the size of Detroit and other manufacturing cities," says Howard P. Segal, professor of history at the University of Maine and author of *Recasting the Machine Age: Henry Ford's Village Industries* (2005).

Ford left the farm for Detroit in 1879 to work as an apprentice to a machinist. He was just sixteen years old. He remained there for three years, eventually returning to Dearborn, where he operated and repaired steam engines, helped overhaul his father's farm equipment, and tried to avoid the farm work he so disliked. After his marriage to Clara Bryant in 1888, Ford ran a sawmill. But industry called, and in 1891 Ford became an engineer with the Edison Illuminating Company. "His genius was in grasping mechanical problems and potential solutions and in hiring others to carry out his ideas," says Segal.

So talented was Ford, in fact, that he was made chief engineer just two years later, which gave him enough money to experiment with internal combustion engines on his own. In 1896, he created a self-propelled four-wheel vehicle called a quadricycle. Cars were next on his agenda, and after a couple of failed attempts to create a car company, he finally succeeded in 1903. "Ford was certainly persistent, and optimistic, about the prospects for manufacturing a car for ordinary Americans. Only Ransom Olds (of Oldsmobile) had similar ideas. All other early American car makers sought only wealthy buyers," Segal wrote in a April 2007 e-mail. Ford did produce a reasonably priced automobile, the Model T, in 1908. It was easy to operate, affordable, and it was soon ubiquitous—by 1918 half of all cars in the United States were Model Ts.

To meet demand, Ford built a large assembly-line factory at Highland Park, Michigan, in 1910. Each worker had a place in line, and added a single component to the car as it traveled along to completion—cars are built much the same way today. The moving assembly line revolutionized automobile production by significantly reducing the amount of time and money it took to build a car. Cheaper cars meant more people could buy them, and this resulted in the Ford Motor Company becoming, for a long time, the largest automobile manufacturer in the world.

According to Howard Segal, Ford "was hardly sophisticated enough to have contemplated, much less to have embraced *The Secret*. There is no evidence that I know of to conclude otherwise. He was a barely literate mechanic who had a facility for mechanics and manufacturing." He also made enough money to indulge his ideas of the assembly line, and therein lie the clues to Ford psyche.

Ford was a pacifist, famous for organizing a Peace Ship in an attempt to stop World War I. The failed boondoggle was widely reported, and ridiculed, at the time. "The Peace Ship shows a naive faith in the ability to prevent or stop war. Andrew Carnegie had similar inclinations, as did some other prominent Americans who were anti-imperialistic. But Ford was viewed as more of a crank (no pun intended) than a serious peace advocate," says Segal. As part of the Peace Ship plan, Ford vowed to "send wireless messages of peace to the men in the trenches, and, while we don't believe that anybody would hold them up, we are sending them on faith—a faith so strong that we believe that they will get through. The two notes that will be sounded are faith and moral suasion," he told a *Times* reporter in a story published on November 28, 1915. On December 1, 1915, the *Times* reported that the Hague would try to suppress the ship if Ford tried to interfere with the war. "In Dutch official circles Henry Ford's proposal to cause a strike in the trenches is characterized as too absurd to merit serious consideration. It is pointed out that any one attempting to foment discontent among soldiers of any of the belligerents would inevitably subject himself to arrest and trial under martial law on a charge of inspiring mutiny."

Something happened on the first ship—dissent among the passengers and illness were both rumored and denied by Ford. Seasickness overtook many passengers, as reported in the *Times* on December 14, 1915. And on December 20, the *Times* reported that dispatches to London newspapers, from reporters on the ship, gave accounts of "exciting squabbles" onboard. Ford even tried to rid the ship of journalists so they would not report on the discontent. In short, it was a public relations and practical disaster. Ford returned, alone, to a south Brooklyn pier on another liner (not the Peace Ship) after the New Year, the *Times* reported on January 3, 1916. "He eluded the newspapermen when the liner docked . . .

but was found three hours later at the Waldorf." That afternoon he consented to an interview, and he told the reporter that the peace expedition was not in danger of collapse because of dissention among the pilgrims onboard, as had been rumored.

On February 7, 1916, Ford announced plans for another ship, the automaker's second attempt at ending the war. A near-endless ability to finance such excursions, and the ability to get media attention for them, echoes the modern activists' model very closely. A rich zealot is hard to stop—yet he did not succeed.

Segal says if Ford believed in the law of attraction, he probably would not have spread anti-Semitic propaganda that was later republished by Adolf Hitler, perhaps because he would have anticipated that those negative thoughts would come back to impact his life in destructive ways. "He did not like the Jews because he believed they were warmongering, manipulative, and alien," writes Neil Baldwin in his biography *Henry Ford and the Jews: The Mass Production of Hate* (2001). Ford was a pacifist who blamed World War I on German Jewish bankers. In the 1920s, he published *The Dearborn Independent,* which featured articles about the Jewish "problem"; these articles are now available in a book called *The International Jew: The World's Problem.* In 1938, he became the first American recipient of a Nazi award given to non-Germans. (The Ford family has put an end to this dark legacy by disowning Ford's beliefs and by supporting Israel and many Jewish charities.)

Ford also blamed the urbanization of America on the Jews—ironically, a situation that *he* helped create. He saw urbanization as a negative, even though he had long disliked farming and rural life. "He tried to reverse urbanization by establishing car plants in nineteen small communities within sixty miles of Dearborn, but these 'village industries,' though relatively pleasant places to work as compared with Ford's huge factories, could not reverse the tide," says Segal. "Ford never understood twentieth-century urban life and spent much time retreating to the one-room schoolhouse and colonial singing and dancing carried on in his Greenfield Village pseudo-historical community not far from Dearborn, site of both his birthplace and Ford world headquarters."

Segal says that if Ford had known and practiced *The Secret,* he also would "not have alienated his once-adoring workers and general public in the 1930s by characterizing the Great Depression as a positive cleansing event." Finally, Segal says that "in middle age, Ford started letting go the brilliant managers, engineers, and advertisers who had done so much to make Ford so rich, so powerful, and so influential, and he began a steady decline that lasted until he died in 1947. He made many friends, to be sure, but he gradually made far more enemies."

If the test of a person's belief and use of the law of attraction is simply that he or she is successful in business for some period of his or her working life, then Ford could qualify, as could Carnegie and certainly Stone, who believed in positive thinking with all his heart. But people are more than the sum of their business success. Stone was by all accounts a happy man, married to the same woman for almost eighty years. Carnegie was also a happy man; Ford, less so. He may not have even completely sane.

These men certainly offer lessons in industry, ingenuity, and passion, whether or not they used a positive mental attitude to realize their achievements. What is most interesting about the "Secret teachers of the past" is how they compare in profession to the "Secret teachers of today." Yesterday's teachers were inventors, scientists, statesmen, manufacturers, and artists who taught through example. In contrast, most of the living teachers of *The Secret* teach the law of attraction in workshops and lectures.

Conclusion

❧

Are We a Secret Society?

PUT ASIDE THE slick packaging and brilliant marketing, scientific claims and psychological theory—and at the end of the day *The Secret* is about the pursuit of happiness. Attaining happiness has been a goal of people worldwide since time began. It is *not* a strictly American goal (although there are certainly unique features to the Yankee propensity for seeking good cheer). And it is a worthy objective, nothing to be ashamed of.

The Secret's take on the subject is squarely aimed at the middle class, and even the affluent among us who feel we should be happier and are convinced that if we were able to assemble all the trappings of a perfect life—lots of money, a big home, a better car, a distinguished career, a *Vogue*-worthy wardrobe, public recognition, and a fairy-tale romance—we'd be content. These are things that seem to make us happy, or at least give us transitory pleasure, which is why we place such a high value on them. The idea that one can accumulate these items simply by thinking about them is appealing in a world where many of us drive, text-message, read the newspaper, eat breakfast, and listen to our favorite music all at the same time. We're busy—who has time to actually *pursue* happiness anymore? It would be so much more convenient if it could just happen while we were dreaming.

Of course, it simply doesn't work that way, for two reasons. First, the law of attraction will frustrate and elude many. It is not going to work for everyone—no matter how positive the thoughts an individual has, he or she may not end up with the desired object or outcome. Second, getting "something for nothing" is not especially satisfying or worthwhile over the long term. A friend of mine from many years ago, a lawyer who devoted himself to advocating for the disabled, liked to say, "Sure, I can give free legal advice, but remember, it is worth precisely what you pay for it. Nothing." A gift bestowed by a friend or family member has talismanic properties because of the giver's sentiment, not the object itself. A dollar found on the street is a lucky discovery; money earned for a job well done is worth more than its face value. If you don't work for something, how much do you really appreciate it?

Losing yourself in the *chase* for happiness, rather than its capture, could be the real key. This is a theme that has threaded its way through this book and has been articulated by the many experts included here. Working at being happy is less effective than working at things you enjoy, that challenge you, or that give you deep satisfaction. Doing what you love may not always result in huge financial gains, but it produces a spiritual and creative fulfillment that outweighs or at least offsets the frustrations and sadness of being overlooked, ignored, or condemned by critics or even colleagues (talk to any artist, musician, or writer who works outside of mainstream tastes and he or she will confirm this). Figuring out why you want to get up in the morning, and then doing it, is much more difficult and scary than aligning yourself with the universe and reading a daily affirmation. Dwelling on what we want all the time can immobilize us and manifest distress.

"You cannot find happiness by purposely searching for it," writes Mihaly Csikszentmihalyi in *Flow: The Psychology of Optimal Experience* (1990). "It is by being fully involved with every detail of our lives, whether good or bad, that we find happiness." He says this can be achieved by getting control over the content of our consciousness, *not to be confused with positive thinking.* "The best moments," he states in the book, "usually occur when a person's body or mind is stretched to the limits in a voluntary effort to accomplish something difficult and worthwhile . . . such experiences are not necessarily pleasant at the time they occur."

So put down your cell phones, unplug your iPod, turn off the TV, tear up your affirmations, and start living.

As Franklin Delano Roosevelt said in his first inaugural address, "Happiness lies not in the mere possession of money; it lies in the joy of achievement, in the thrill of creative effort."

Further Reading

The following list is by no means exhaustive. If your favorite books on Buddhism or Beethoven are not included here, please don't be offended. This list has been selected based on advice from experts, and my own research, as a beginning resource for many of the topics covered in this book. I have listed books, whenever possible, in editions readily available today. Most are still in print; those that are not can be bought used at Web sites such as AbeBooks.com, Alibris.com, Amazon.com, BN.com, and Powells.com. The studies listed are available from the archives of the journals where they appeared.

Christian Socialism and New Thought Writers and Critics

Behrend, Genevieve, with Joe Vitale. *How to Attain Your Desires by Letting Your Subconscious Mind Work for You, Vol. 1.* Garden City, N.Y.: Morgan James Publishing, 2004. Behrend's book appeared originally under the title *Attaining Your Desires by Letting Your Subconscious Mind Work for You.*

Collier, Robert. *Be Rich! The Science of Getting What You Want.* Oak Harbor, Wash.: Robert Collier Publishing, 1970.

———. *The Secret of the Ages.* 1917. Repr. New York: Pocketbook/ Robert Collier Publishing, 1978.

Crunden, Robert M. *Ministers of Reform: The Progressives' Achievement in American Civilization 1889–1920.* Chicago: University of Illinois Press, 1985.

Haanel, Charles. *The Master Key System.* 1916. Repr. Whitefish, Mont.: Kessinger Publishing, 2003. Available at www.psitek.net.

Herron, George D. *The Christian State: A Political Vision of Christ.* 1895. Repr. Boston, Mass.: Adamant Media Corporation, 2001.

Hill, Napoleon. *Law of Success, The 21st Century Edition.* 1928. Repr. Arden, N.C.: High Roads Media, 2004.

———. *Think and Grow Rich: The Original Version, Restored and Revised,* 1937. Repr. San Diego, Calif.: Aventine Press, 2004.

Huxley, Aldous. *Brave New World.* 1932. Repr. New York: Harper Perennial Modern Classics, 1998.

James, William. *The Principles of Psychology* 1890. Available online at psychclassics.yorku.ca/James/Principles/index.htm.

———. *The Varieties of Religious Experience.* 1902. Repr. Charleston, S.C.: BiblioBazaar, 2007.

———. *The Will to Believe.* 1896. Repr. New York: Cosimo, 2006.

Marden, Orison Swett. *How to Get What You Want.* 1917. Repr. Champaign, Ill.: Book Jungle, 2006.

———. *Pushing to the Front.* 1894. Repr. New York: Cosimo, 2005.

Meyer, Donald. *The Positive Thinkers: Popular Religious Psychology from Mary Baker Eddy to Norman Vincent Peale and Ronald Reagan.* Middletown, Conn.: Wesleyan University Press, 1988.

Peale, Norman Vincent. *The Power of Positive Thinking.* 1952. Repr. New York: Ballantine Books, 1996.

Satter, Beryl. *Each Mind a Kingdom: Women, Sexual Purity, and the New Thought Movement, 1875–1920.* Berkeley, Calif.: University of California Press, 2001.

Towne, Elizabeth. *Experiences in Self-Healing.* 1905. Repr. New York: Cosimo, 2007.

———. *Joy Philosophy.* 1903. Repr. Whitefish, Mont.: Kessinger Publishing, 2004.

Wattles, Wallace. *The Science of Getting Rich.* 1910. Repr. Rockford, Ill.: BN Publishing, 2006.

Media and Culture

Belton, John. *American Cinema/American Culture.* 2nd ed. New York: McGraw-Hill, 2004.
———. *Movies and Mass Culture.* London: Athlone Press, 1999.
Jenkins, Henry. *Convergence Culture: Where Old and New Media Collide.* New York: New York University Press, 2006.
Kremer, John. *1001 Ways to Market Your Book.* 6th ed. Taos, N.Mex.: Open Horizons, 2006.

Psychology and Sociology

Csikszentmihalyi, Mihaly. *Flow: The Psychology of Optimal Experience.* New York: HarperCollins, 1990.
Langer, Ellen J. *Mindfulness.* Boston, Mass.: Addison Wesley, 1990.
———. *On Becoming an Artist: Reinventing Yourself Through Mindful Creativity.* New York: Ballantine Books, 2006.
———. *The Power of Mindful Learning.* New York: Perseus, 1998.
Seligman, M. E. P. *Learned Optimism.* New York: Pocket Books, 1998.
Twenge, Jean M. *Generation Me: Why Today's Young Americans Are More Confident, Assertive, Entitled—and More Miserable Than Ever Before.* New York: Free Press, 2007.

Placebo and Positive Thinking Research on Health

The journal studies listed here are only a fraction of the research that has been done on psychology and health.

BOOKS
Brody, Howard, with Daralyn Brody. *The Placebo Response: How You Can Release the Body's Inner Pharmacy for Better Health.* New York: Harper Perennial, 2001.

STUDIES

Duckworth, A. L., and M. E. P. Seligman. 2006. "Self-Discipline Outdoes IQ in Predicting Academic Performance of Adolescents." *Psychological Science* 16(12): 939–944.

Fitzgerald, T. E., et al. 1993. "The Relative Importance of Dispositional Optimism and Control Appraisals in Quality of Life After Coronary Bypass Surgery." *Journal of Behavioral Medicine* 16: 25–43.

Gillham, J. E., and M. E. P. Seligman. 1999. "Footsteps on the Road to Positive Psychology." *Behaviour Research and Therapy* 37: S163–S173.

Isaacowitz, D. M., G. E. Vaillant, and M. E. P. Seligman. 2003. "Strengths and Satisfaction Across the Adult Lifespan." *International Journal of Aging and Human Development* 57(2): 181–201.

Peterson, C., N. Park, and M. E. P. Seligman. 2006. "Greater Strengths of Character and Recovery from Illness." *Journal of Positive Psychology* 1(1): 17–26.

———. 2005. "Orientations to Happiness and Life Satisfaction: The Full Life Versus the Empty Life." *Journal of Happiness Studies* 6(1): 25–41.

———. 2004. "Reply: Strengths of Character and Well-Being: A Closer Look at Hope and Modesty." *Journal of Social and Clinical Psychology* 23(5): 628–634.

———. 2004. "Strengths of Character and Well-Being." *Journal of Social and Clinical Psychology* 23: 603–619.

Robinson-Whelan, S., et al. 1997. "Distinguishing Optimism from Pessimism in Older Adults: Is It More Important to Be Optimistic or Not to Be Pessimistic?" *Journal of Personality and Social Psychology* 73: 1345–1353.

Scheier, M. F., and C. S. Carver. 1992. "Effects of Optimism on Psychological and Physical Well-Being: Theoretical Overview and Empirical Update." *Cognitive Therapy and Research* 16: 201–228.

———, and M. W. Bridges. 1994. "Distinguishing Optimism from Neuroticism (and Trait Anxiety, Self-Mastery, and Self-Esteem: A Reevaluation of the Life Orientation Test." *Journal of Personality and Social Psychology* 67: 1063–1078.

Physics

Albert, David Z. *Quantum Mechanics and Experience and Time and Chance.* Cambridge, Mass.: Harvard University Press, 1994.

Capra, Fritjof. *Eastern Mysticism.* Boston, Mass.: Shambhala, 2000.

Einstein, Albert. *Relativity: The General and the Special Theory.* New York: Penguin Classics, 2006.

Feynman, Richard P. *Surely You're Joking, Mr. Feynman! Adventures of a Curious Character.* New York: W. W. Norton, 1997.

———, Robert B. Leighton, and Matthew Sands. *The Feynman Lectures on Physics: The Definitive and Extended Edition.* 2nd ed. Boston, Mass.: Addison Wesley, 2005.

Griffiths, Robert B. *Consistent Quantum Theory.* Cambridge, England: Cambridge University Press, 2004.

Hawking, Stephen. *A Brief History of Time.* 10th anniversary edition. New York: Bantam, 1998.

———. *God Created the Integers: The Mathematical Breakthroughs That Changed History.* Philadelphia, Penn.: Running Press Book Publishers, 2005.

———. *The Universe in a Nutshell.* New York: Bantam, 2001.

Penrose, Roger. *Shadows of the Mind: A Search for the Missing Science of Consciousness.* New York: Oxford University Press, 1996.

———. *The Emperor's New Mind: Concerning Computers, Minds, and the Laws of Physics.* New York: Oxford University Press, 2002.

———. *The Road to Reality: A Complete Guide to the Laws of the Universe.* New York: Vintage, 2007.

———, Stephen Hawking, et al. *The Large, the Small and the Human Mind.* Cambridge, England: Cambridge University Press, 2000.

Stenger, Victor J. *The Unconscious Quantum: Metaphysics in Modern Physics and Cosmology.* Amherst, N.Y.: Prometheus Books, 1995.

Wolf, Fred Alan. *The Tao of Physics: An Exploration of the Parallels Between Modern Physics and Taking the Quantum Leap.* Rev. ed. New York: Harper Perennial, 1989.

Zukav, Gary. *The Dancing Wu Li Masters.* New York: Harper Perennial Modern Classics, 2001.

Brain Science

Begley, Sharon. *Train Your Mind, Change Your Brain: How a New Science Reveals Our Extraordinary Potential to Transform Ourselves.* New York: Ballantine Books, 2007.

Bremner, J. Douglas. *Does Stress Damage the Brain? Understanding Trauma-Related Disorders from a Mind-Body Perspective.* New York: W. W. Norton, 2005.

Doidge, Norman. *The Brain That Changes Itself: Stories of Personal Triumph from the Frontiers of Brain Science.* New York: Viking, 2007.

Religion

CHRISTIANITY

Johnson, Paul. *A History of Christianity.* New York: Touchstone, 1979.

Lewis, C. S. *Mere Christianity.* San Francisco: HarperSanFrancisco, 2001.

Thomas, Oliver. *10 Things Your Minister Wants to Tell You (But Can't, Because He Needs the Job).* New York: St. Martin's Press, 2007.

JEWISH MYSTICISM

Cohen-Sherbok, Dan. *Kabbalah and Jewish Mysticism: An Introductory Anthology.* Oxford, England: Oneworld Publications, 2006.

Dennis, Geoffrey W. *Encyclopedia of Jewish Myth, Magic and Mysticism.* Woodbury, Minn.: Llewellyn, 2007.

BUDDHISM

Seager, Richard. *Buddhism in America.* New York: Columbia University Press, 2000.

———. *Buddhist Humanism.* Berkeley, Calif.: University of California Press, 2006.

Suzuki, D. T. *Encountering the Dharma: Daisaku Ikeda, Soka Gakkai, and the Globalization of an Introduction to Zen Buddhism.* New York: Grove Press, 1994.

CHRISTIAN SCIENCE

Cather, Willa, and Georgine Milmine. *The Life of Mary Baker G. Eddy and the History of Christian Science.* 1909. Repr. Lincoln, Neb.: University of Nebraska Press, 1993.

Eddy, Mary Baker. *Science and Health with Key to the Scriptures.* 1875. Repr. Boston, Mass.: Writings of Mary Baker Eddy Publishing, 1984.

Biographies

LUDWIG VAN BEETHOVEN

Forbes, Elliot, ed. *Thayer's Life of Beethoven.* Rev. ed. Princeton, N.J.: Princeton University Press, 1973.

Schindler, Anton Felix. *Beethoven As I Knew Him.* New York: Dover Books, 1996.

Solomon, Maynard. *Beethoven.* 2nd rev. ed. New York: Schirmer Trade Books, 2001.

Sonneck, O. G., ed. *Beethoven Impressions by His Contemporaries.* New York: Dover Books, 1967.

Sullivan, J. W. N. *Beethoven: His Spiritual Development.* 1927. Repr. Whitefish, Mont.: Kessinger Publishing, 2003.

WILLIAM SHAKESPEARE

Dutton, Richard. *William Shakespeare: A Literary Life.* New York: Macmillan, 1989.

Greenblatt, Stephen. *Will in the World: How Shakespeare Became Shakespeare.* New York: W. W. Norton, 2004.

Honan, Park. *Shakespeare: A Life.* New York: Oxford University Press, 1998.

Nuttall, A. D. *Shakespeare the Thinker.* New Haven, Conn.: Yale University Press, 2007.

Schoenbaum, S. *William Shakespeare: A Compact Documentary Life.* New York: Oxford University Press, 1977.

RALPH WALDO EMERSON

Emerson, Ralph Waldo. *Emerson's Prose and Poetry: A Reader.* New York: W. W. Norton, 2001.

Geldard, Richard. *The Spiritual Teachings of Ralph Waldo Emerson.* 2nd rev. ed. Great Barrington, Mass.: Lindisfarne Books, 2001.

Myerson, Joel, ed. *Transcendentalism: A Reader.* New York: Oxford University Press, 2000.

THOMAS EDISON

Baldwin, Neil. *Edison: Inventing the Century.* New York: Hyperion, 1995.

Bryan, George S. *Edison: The Man and His Work.* New York: Alfred A. Knopf, 1926.

Israel, Paul. *Edison: A Life of Invention.* Hoboken, N.J.: Wiley, 2000.

Stross, Randall E. *The Wizard of Menlo Park: How Thomas Alva Edison Invented the Modern World.* New York: Crown, 2007.

WINSTON CHURCHILL

Churchill, Winston. *My Early Life: 1874–1904.* 1930. Repr. New York: Touchstone, 1996.

Keegan, John. *Winston Churchill.* New York: Penguin Lives, 2002.

ALBERT EINSTEIN

Clark, Ronald W. *Einstein: The Life and Times.* New York: Harper Perennial, 2007.

Einstein, Albert. *Ideas and Opinions.* 1955. Repr. London: Souvenir Press, 2005.

————, with Banesh Hoffman and Helen Dukas, eds. *Albert Einstein: The Human Side.* Princeton, N.J.: Princeton University Press, 1979.

Isaacson, Walter. *Einstein: His Life and Universe.* New York: Simon and Schuster, 2007.

Overbye, Dennis. *Einstein in Love: A Scientific Romance.* New York: Penguin, 2001.

ANDREW CARNEGIE

Carnegie, Andrew, and Gordon Hutner. *The Autobiography of Andrew Carnegie and the Gospel of Wealth.* New York: Signet Classics, 2006.

Nasaw, David. *Andrew Carnegie.* New York: Penguin, 2006.

HENRY FORD

Ford, Henry. *The International Jew: The World's Foremost Problem.* 1920–1922. Repr. Reedy, W.Va.: Liberty Bell Publications, 2004.

————. *My Life and Work.* 1926. Available online at www.gutenberg.org.

Segal, Howard P. *Recasting the Machine Age: Henry Ford's Village Industries.* Amherst, Mass.: University of Massachusetts Press, 2005.

Acknowledgments

Writing this book has been an extraordinarily enlightening personal journey, and many people helped me en route. First, I want to thank Madeleine Morel at 2M Communications, not only for her belief in my abilities but for her encouragement, good counsel, and sense of humor. Many, many thanks to the publisher, Thomas Dunne, who posed a question and allowed me the privilege of answering it. Erin Brown is the best editor ever; she took my hand and jumped right into the deep end of the pool with me. Her Southern hospitality made me feel as if I had known her all my life.

The incredible people at St. Martin's exemplify the true meaning of teamwork: thank you to Martha Cameron for her amazing copyediting; legal eagles Diana Frost and Surie Rudoff; production editor Julie Gutin; and managing editor Amelie Littell.

So many authentically learned and knowledgeable scholars, scientists, psychologists, doctors, philosophers, filmmakers, theologians, writers, and journalists very graciously, and with good cheer, shared their time and insights with me, and helped me understand more about their fields. These generous souls all deserve special mention (in alphabetical order):

Virgil E. Barnes, Ph.D., Purdue University
Sharon Begley, *Newsweek*
J. Douglas Bremner, Ph.D., Emory University
Howard Brody, M.D., Institute for the Medical Humanities at the University of Texas Medical Branch
Alice Calaprice
Betsy Chasse
John Demartini
Rabbi Geoffrey Dennis, Congregation Kol Ami in Flower Mound, Texas
Norman Doidge, M.D., University of Toronto and Columbia University
David Felten, M.D., Ph.D., Beaumont Research Institute
Arielle Ford, the Ford Sisters and the Spiritual Cinema Circle
John Gray
Robert Griffiths, Ph.D., Carnegie-Mellon University
Henry Jenkins, Ph.D., Massachusetts Institute of Technology
Ben Johnson, M.D.
Gail Jones
John Kremer
Ellen Langer, Ph.D., Harvard University
Robert L. Leahy, Ph.D., Weill Medical College at Cornell University
Joel Myerson, Ph.D., University of South Carolina
David Nasaw, Ph.D., City University of New York
Sara Nelson, *Publishers Weekly*

Dennis Overbye, *The New York Times*
Kristine Pidkameny, One Spirit Book Club
Camille Ricketts, *The Wall Street Journal*
Allen Salkin, *The New York Times*
Connie Sayre, Market Partners International
Richard Seager, Ph.D., Hamilton College
Howard Segal, Ph.D., University of Maine
Darren Sherkat, Ph.D., Southern Illinois University at Carbondale
Laura Smith, Lime Radio
Alan Sokal, Ph.D., New York University
Lee Spector, Ph.D., Hampshire College
Phillips Stevens Jr., State University of New York at Buffalo
John Suler, Ph.D., Rider University
Pastor Oliver "Buzz" Thomas
Jean Twenge, Ph.D., San Diego State University
Priscilla Wald, Ph.D., Duke University
Clifford M. Will, Ph.D., Washington University
Fred Alan Wolf

A very special thank-you to Susan Kelly, Ph.D., medieval scholar and adjunct professor of literary journalism at Hampshire College, and my wonderful sister, for invaluable help accessing archives and research on historical figures, and for thoughts on Shakespearean drama and Elizabethan philosophy; Randy Sandke, musician and music historian, and beloved husband, for the use of his extensive Beethoven library and for making important insights into the composer's life, work, and philosophy, and for his observations concerning Thomas Edison and the early recording industry (and for playing examples of Edison records on Edison players); and John Belton, professor of English and Film at

Rutgers University, adviser, film scholar, and friend, for sharing his views on film theory and American culture.

There are a handful of steadfast family, friends, and colleagues who offer continuous inspiration, moral support, and general cheerleading, especially important when undertaking a book project. They are the "secret" to my success: my dear parents, William and Constance Kelly; my sister Nancy Kelly and brother William Kelly; Claudia Cross at Sterling Lord Literistic; Charles Winecoff; Mary Bolster; Bonnie Bauman; C. Claiborne Ray; Mauro DiPreta; Janis Spindel; Marta Tracy; Terence Noonan; and all my sisters in P.E.O. NY Chapter R.

A final shoutout goes to my two muses and constant companions: Puff Daddy and Julius. Meow!

GARFIELD COUNTY
LIBRARIES
www.gcpld.org